SOUND

Profound Experiences with Chanting, Toning, Music, and Healing Frequencies

Enjoy these other books in the Common Sentience series:

ANCESTORS: *Divine Remembrances of Lineage, Relations and Sacred Sites*

ANGELS: *Personal Encounters with Divine Beings of Light*

ANIMALS: *Personal Tales of Encounters with Spirit Animals*

ASCENSION: *Divine Stories of Awakening the Whole and Holy Being Within*

GUIDES: *Mystical Connections to Soul Guides and Divine Teachers*

MEDITATION: *Intimate Experiences with the Divine through Contemplative Practices*

NATURE: *Divine Experiences with Trees, Plants, Stones and Landscapes*

SHAMANISM: *Personal Quests of Communion with Nature and Creation*

SIGNS: *Sacred Encounters with Pathways, Turning Points, and Divine Guideposts*

Learn more at sacredstories.com.

SOUND

Profound Experiences with Chanting, Toning, Music, and Healing Frequencies

DRS. J.J. & DESIREE HURTAK

SACRED STORIES
PUBLISHING

Books may be purchased through booksellers or by contacting Sacred Stories Publishing.

Cymatics Photo Credit (c) 2023 Sacred Resonance www.sacredresonance.com.au.

To listen to the sacred sounds and meditations visit https://sacredstories.com/commonsentience-sound.

Sound:
Profound Experiences with Chanting, Toning, Music, and Healing Frequencies

Drs. J.J. Hurtak, Ph.D., Ph.D., M.Th. and Desiree Hurtak, Ph.D.

Print ISBN: 978-1-958921-23-4
EBook ISBN: 978-1-958921-24-1

Library of Congress Control Number: 2023934024

Published by Sacred Stories Publishing, Fort Lauderdale, FL USA

CONTENTS

PART THREE: DEEPENING YOUR EXPERIENCE WITH SOUND

PART ONE

Understanding Sound

There is geometry in the humming of the strings.
There is music in the spacing of the spheres.

—PYTHAGORAS

THE GREAT SONG OF A LIVING UNIVERSE

s human beings, we fully resonate with sound, be it our favorite poem or song or even the voice of someone we love to hear. Yes, we are visual people, but we also respond to sound, especially music, which has been found to exist throughout human cultures, as seen in the very early Neanderthal flutes, with the oldest found in Slovenia. These flutes were made from bird bones, and date back some 60,000 years. In our youth, we learned to mimic sounds, and as we grow old, our favorite music can be used to re-awaken our minds.

Our brains are hardwired to respond to sounds, and also to help us to create musical tones through our voices. There is, however, much more to sound than that which we can produce and our ears can hear. Sound is everywhere and in everything that is alive and in some things that are not. Our body itself is a collection of resonating vibratory frequencies. Each organ produces soundscapes that resonate together, creating a biological chorus within us. In short, every part of the human body modulates sounds intentionally like a built-in set of micro-composers creating music. We are clearly "sound boards," and our body is indeed a "Body Electric," resonating music throughout itself, right down to our DNA.

Understanding this power, the Pythagoreans used music to heal the body and to elevate the soul as they understood how we were connected with the universal "Music of the Spheres." Still today, the power of sound for healing of body and mind continues in our modern world in various acoustic modalities.

What exactly is sound? Sound can be measured as various frequencies expressed in Hertz (Hz), which define the number of sound vibrations in one second of time, so if you have a string operating at 440 Hz, it moves at 440 vibrations per second. It was Pythagoras who further discovered that the "pitch" of a sound can be related to the length of a string producing the sound, namely the shorter the string the higher the pitch.

It is important to know at the onset that we hear sounds around us in a very narrow band of approximately 20 Hz to 20,000 Hz (20 kHz), while elephants are one of the few species that can hear sounds lower than we can at 16 Hz, which is into the "infrasound" range, below our human audibility. Dogs and cats can go up to 45,000 Hz and 64,000 Hz, respectively. Porpoises have even a higher range reaching 150,000 Hz or more. Bats also hear at higher ranges of the sound spectrum from 9,000 Hz -200,000 Hz. Mice fall within the higher ranges as well, often making sounds we cannot hear.

Music is created from sounds we can hear, but not all audible sound is necessarily music! However, whether we can hear it or not, sound is basically a tone or frequency. Whenever any animal or human emits a sound, it causes the surrounding air molecules to vibrate, initiating "sound wave vibrations" as a pressure wave, moving through air. It emerges on a specific frequency range, and that can be received by the human ear only when it is "loud" enough, which is at about 10 dB. Normal conversation is about 50 dB, and a siren is about 120 dB.

Plants and planets can also make sounds through "electrical resonant" vibrations that can easily be transferred to audible signals that we can enjoy as music. In our personal work over the last forty-five years, we have covered the gamut of sound from Indigenous singers in Brazil to the American jazz artist Alice Coltrane, all of whom have used their skills of composition and instrumentation along with the human voice to sing ancient, Sacred Expressions that have inspired millions of people. We have also used sound testing equipment with such musical experts as Alan Howarth who worked on the movie *Halloween* and composed some of the special music effects for the *Star Trek* motion picture series. By using computer-sound recording equipment with Howarth, we have recorded the resonance in the Pyramids of Mexico and the principal pyramids and temples of Egypt. That is, we generated pink (ambient) noise and white (broadband) noise to record the "archeo-acoustics" of the inner and outer structures of these ancient sacred sites, as well as that of the voice sounding within them.

"Archeo-acoustics" is research involving the architecture of ancient cultures, mainly within their temples or tombs, but also the exterior of these complexes, because sometimes the temples were made to resonate throughout the entirety of the stone structure (e.g., Chichen Itza and Tikal). We tested the harmonic resonances of many of these temples. In our tests, there was seldom just a single sound that was recorded on our devices. Instead, there were single sounds and harmonies of sound that were also harmonics or frequencies that blended or resonated together.

What determines the harmonics of a sound? If we vibrate a string on a cello, for example, or any string instrument, and lightly touch it exactly midway between the bridge and the nut, a particular tone is produced that is one octave higher than the fundamental open string. This is called the second harmonic with a frequency ratio of 2:1. That is to say, it has twice the frequency of the fundamental pitch.

If we now touch the string at another point or 1/3 of the string length, yet another harmonic sound is created, and the string vibrates in three sections. If you want to sound the fourth harmonic, you would touch the vibrating string at the node which is located at 1/4 of the string's total length. The third and second harmonics have a ratio of 3:2, which gives us the interval of a perfect fifth. The fourth and third harmonics have a ratio of 4:3, which gives us the relationship of a perfect fourth. The octave can also be divided, for example, into the fifth and by inversion of the fourth. If you use the term "overtone," then typically you have the fundamental pitch, and then the "first overtone" is at the octave above the fundamental.

Although harmonic patterns were also understood by Pythagoras as he had discovered the mathematical basis of harmony, the mathematician Hermann Helmholtz took this one step further to determine consonant harmonics which are pleasant to hear and dissonant intervals which are not. These dissonant intervals tend to create tension or instability. For example, by tossing a 10-pound rock into a pond, and then throwing a 20-pound rock in after it—you can see the ripples of the waves harmonize, just like playing two notes an octave apart. But if instead you threw in a 10-pound rock and then a 16-pound rock, the waves would conflict. This is the notion that Helmholtz talked about regarding consonance and dissonance, which is further related to the Fibonacci sequence.

Each fundamental which is the lowest tone in the harmonic series, or the root tone, produces harmonics, and according to the instrument being used, these harmonics are produced in different frequencies (Hz) and intensities (dB). Yet, if a guitar and a piano each play the same note, which is the fundamental, how can we tell them apart? One would say, by the quality of the sound. Technically, it is related to the instrument you play—the same harmonics of a string can be known by its quality or timbre which is due to the relative mass of each instrument (or bow) producing it. Therefore, another key element of what makes each sound unique, what helps to impart timbre, is the unique pattern of resonances among its harmonics.

All this has a parallel in the scientific understanding of light, where waves are "coherent" with each other if they have exactly the same range of wavelengths and the same phase differences at their wavelengths. Waves in consonance tend to enhance each other. Overall, there is clearly a relationship between sound and light. Color, too, works with the frequencies of both sound and light, but a discussion of that will be saved for a few words later in this book. There are also frequencies that we will discuss in this book including the Schumann resonance and certain forms of brainwave entrainment that can be analyzed especially through electronic means.

Yet, why is it important to learn more about music and sound? Why not just enjoy popular music easily available on the internet, or for some, go back to the classics of an earlier period? Well, researchers all over the world are finding that we are really living bio-antennas and that music or sounds, like those in nature, can help heal us.

Our body is, in effect, a large collection of vibratory systems that are both antennae/receivers and senders of vibrations. These and other vibrations can be used for either renewal and regeneration of life or its destruction. If we truly understand this, then we realize that music can help relieve stress and establish within us a state of relaxation, which can calm our heart rate and help reduce our blood pressure, but equally important, help us in our endeavors to reach higher states of consciousness and inner peace. Some sounds or even inaudible frequencies, however, can do just the opposite!

Studies have shown that classical music playing in the background can actually facilitate learning and help us to achieve higher states of creativity. Some people have used certain music to stop smoking while others have analyzed it for interspecies communications. Music may be one of the missing links spanning from soul evolution to science.

The Keys of Enoch® initiated a genre of vibratory linkages called "axiatonal music" that helps to create links connecting the body, mind, and soul. It is a music that is collectively generated from the biological networks, including the small microtubules and bio-geometries within our body, and then extended into our consciousness which brings forth a Divine Awareness and can assist us in healing the "Body Electric." In short, these bio-resonant frequencies can help us to achieve what the ancient texts refer to as the "rainbow body" or "light body" that was said to merge the human resonance field of vibration back into the Light.

One of the goals of this book is to help others understand the whole vibratory pattern of our body and how the human *chakras* can act as nodal points to communicate with the energy fields around us and our Higher Selves. Therefore, it is designed not only to dialog on the importance of sound and music in our lives but also to help us realize that sound healing could equally be used for stress reduction or for broadcasting a "hello" to life forms in outer space via the Voyager space probes and the SETI (Search for ET Intelligence) programs, or to even go further and make contact with those of Higher Consciousness realities living in various other dimensional realms.

A new page of music is now also tuning us into a brighter future through the sounds of the human heart meeting the sensitive feelings of our plants and our animal relatives. What researchers in the United States, Australia, and Italy have found is that plants, animals, and people all share a common need for healing, communication, and a living inter-species fellowship. Since all life is based on inter-dependency, our connections come not just from our ability to react to chemical substances but also from "feeling" the light and colors emitted by life around us as we all learn to better communicate with each other.

We are told we have come out of the primordial sound, whether it be the OM or the *Logos* (the Word), yet now we need to begin to hear the "Cry of Mother Earth" and to join the world of musical experience in actively using positive sounds, sometimes incorporating ancient Sacred Expressions, in cities and sacred places around the world to create a better harmonic of life. Forged as a cooperative effort, these vibrational frequencies as musical notes can be used to construct a more harmonious Song of Co-Creation.

To paraphrase Carlos Santana, we are here to proclaim the "Universal Tone" of Life! In the view of the authors, the time has come to ascend to a new positive vibratory frequency. We must listen and realize we are all musical instruments in the great song of a Living Universe. As Plato tells us: "It [music] gives soul to the universe, wings to the mind, flight to the imagination, and life to everything."

PLANT MUSIC
A SYMPHONIC SYNERGY

— ∞ —

t has been understood for generations that sounds act on the neurons and structures of the brain, both in animals and humans, creating synaptic connections between cells. In fact, a good portion of anything we learn comes from a complex exchange of information through sound. Sound also influences our memories. However, according to Suzanne Simard, who is a Professor of Forest Ecology at the University of British Columbia, and others like best-selling author and forester, Peter Wohlleben, in plants, there are no brains or central nervous systems, yet they can still receive and send "sound" vibrations. They seem to have their own signaling pathways that function in learning and memory by means of electrical and chemical stimuli. It was originally thought that communication between plants could only be chemical or magnetic but, in fact, much of their communication and even patterns of growth seem to be via sound, especially sounds that mimic nature.

Humanity, sadly, no longer has a deep relationship with the plant world. Yet, as the extraordinary movie, *Avatar*, created by James Cameron, portrayed, there is a deep relationship between Mother Earth and all of nature as an integral part of the earth life-force that can "communicate" with us with both the power of the mind and also by sound. Many studies at the

Biodesign Institute at Arizona State University have shown that plants are endowed with greater abilities of perception, memory, and communication than we had previously realized. In accordance with the theory of evolution, it is feasible that there may be plants with different degrees of intelligence, the study of which requires an entirely new type of discipline called "plant neurobiology." Moreover, plants seem to have elements related to our neurotransmitters such as serotonin, dopamine, and glutamate, although their function is not yet clear.

Those involved in laboratory tests with music and plants have noticed that the roots of the young plants grow in the direction of certain musical sounds. In fact, the root system seems to play a key part in their overall system, just as portrayed in the inspiring film, *Avatar*. Plants are also not as individualistic as we thought. When you place them in larger fields, the larger plants seem to try to support the younger ones.

Avatar provided us, through the story of the Na'vi people and the Great Mother who inspires, sustains, remembers, heals, and receives souls as they arrive and depart, with a glimpse into a possible future of harmony and awareness for humankind, while also tapping into very ancient memories of Shamanism. Shamans around the world have always revered trees as sacred, for the energies they preserve both of ancient and recent past memories.

We worked directly with the late Dr. Marcel Vogel, the IBM scientist who helped to develop the magnetic recording strips for high-speed discs and developed black lights that were popular in the 1960s—who was overall a multi-talented man whose work on plant communication was equally world-renowned. His research with Christopher Bird was some of the greatest conducted in this field, presenting unique and unprecedented opportunities to cross scientific boundaries, and to use the power of the mind literally to communicate with plants. They were able to affirm that plants function in a sentient way both within their surroundings and with us. However, in addition to plants' reactions to our thoughts, they began to see that plants also clearly react to sounds.

In the book *The Secret Life of Plants,* authors and researchers Christopher Bird and Peter Tompkins show that numerous forms of plant life can and do communicate with humans and cite how sound, even some form of musical score, can be received and reacted to by the plants. This book, published in 1973, became a bestseller, which indicated that a new awareness was emerging. It cites many scholars like Mary Measures and Pearl Weinberger who wrote in the Canadian scientific journal, *Botany,* in the 1970s that "sound waves might produce a resonant effect in the plant cells, enabling the energy to accumulate and affect the plant's metabolism." They used 300 Hz, 5 kHz, 1250 Hz, and 12 kHz frequencies and found that the first two frequencies helped plant growth while the last two did not.[1]

Another article entitled "Acoustic and magnetic communication in plants: Is it possible?" by Monica Gagliano and colleagues, published in the journal *Plant Signaling & Behavior* (2012), showed that their research on *Capsicum annuum* (chili peppers) indicated that plants can sense their neighbors and that they signal back and forth through waveforms of both electromagnetic (e.g., extremely low frequency magnetic fields such as Schumann resonances) and acoustic wave forms.[2] Although these findings are still controversial, such acoustic waves were considered by Gagliano, *et. al.* to be "generated as a result of mechanical vibrations of charged cell membranes and walls" along with chemical energy derived from the hydrolysis of ATP in actin filaments which can generate mechanical vibrations within cells. These cells work in a collective mode that can lead to acoustic flows in the order of 150–200 kHz.

When most of us think about plants around our home, we tend to think of them as relics from a simpler, pre-human evolutionary past, but not as a form of intelligent life; however, when we start to work with plants with a greater awareness, we begin to realize that they have a secret life that may even be stranger and more wonderful than the one described by Peter Tompkins and

Christopher Bird. Whether we examine the work of Marcel Vogel or read *The Secret Life of Plants*, which includes the research of L. George Lawrence with his psycho-galvanic analyzer, we come to realize that plants as a life form are "aware" of their surroundings, of each other and of us.

In about 1973, Dorothy Retallack, conducting her research at Colorado Women's College in Denver, began her own experiments with plants using different types of sound and, ultimately, music. She is probably best known for playing "rock" music by such popular artists as Jimi Hendrix and Led Zeppelin to her plants. The plants eventually leaned away from the hard rock music regardless of the light source that they would normally lean towards.

Our extensive discussions with Vogel, Lawrence, Tompkins, Bird, and other friends emphasized music as the key to vitality and regenesis. We are nourished by plants as our food source, yet we can also nourish them with both light and music.

With this in mind, another researcher worth mentioning here is Dr. T.C. Singh from the Department of Botany at Annamalai University in India, who began to wonder whether sound, properly dispersed, could increase the annual harvest of crops. From 1960 to 1963, he piped the Charukesi Raga, as well as other musical compositions, by means of a loud-speaker to six varieties of rice at different stages of growth, generally in fields in the state of Madras and in Pondicherry. The resulting harvests clearly showed an increase in growth from 25 - 60 percent higher than average.

Singh's intention was to help farmers and those in food production be better prepared to use music signals that could be translated into plant growth, as well as assist in the removal of insects. The work of these dedicated researchers using sound, although working independently, has discovered a resonant field for plant growth that can be used to increase the energy field of plants' food production.

Currently, our associate, Jim Dilettoso, founder of Village Labs (Arizona) is continuing research in this field with his BioMolecular Simulation and sonification. Dilettoso is a technical genius, composer, and passionate researcher who has worked with numerous experts from Michael Pinder of the *Moody Blues*, to various NASA scientists. Ultimately, he also spent years decoding plant reactions with top ecologists and experimented to determine what sounds best stimulated plant growth. He determined that it was not a single sound that was effective, but rather a resonance of sound, much like a bird's chirp that was more part of a cavity of sound or insect sounds that activated the growth, and especially stimulated the ATP in plants. In other words, sounds that mimic those found in nature are most effective. Dilettoso's depth of experience from working with single pots of plants to 10,000 acres of organic food crops provides some important keys in the understanding of the type of relationship that can be created with plants using what he calls "Agrisonix," as plants also seem to have different musical resonant frequencies.

Jim told us in personal conversations about the music of the plants: "Silica, quartz, it is everywhere, in the earth and plants … and when the sound stimulates the silica that is in the plant, the piezoelectric effect happens making a slight tiny voltage that is released in the roots. What good is that? Well overall the music triggers within the ATP of the plant which stimulates growth."

Dilettoso went so far as to build a type of *terrasphere* [curved plastic pot] to generate the specific frequency sounds required. His research somewhat paralleled Dan Carlson's "Sonic Bloom," and several others who continue to affirm that certain sound waves can stimulate plant growth, activating their ATP. It is also thought that the piezoelectric part of the plant's rhizome system is being activated. Additionally, specific sounds are thought to stimulate the movement of nutrients throughout the plants' structure, as well as helping to stimulate their immune system. So, playing sounds to plants, whether in pots or in soil, has been shown to enhance their growing experience.

Currently, numerous researchers are working behind-the-scenes in applying the best modern, advanced sound generating instruments to discern the appropriate frequencies necessary to develop a sustainable permaculture using sound and ultrasound. Research into the sound signals or music of the plants is not intended simply to be fun research, but to create a productive application to benefit agriculture. In the larger tradition of sound and environment, shamans and farmers have always known that plant growth is influenced and stimulated by other neighboring plants and also by the sounds produced by shamans using shells and other objects on their clothing as they walk or dance in the fields, plus, of course, the additional sounds of birds and insects.

Legends from all over the world, on every continent and in every age, speak of sentient trees, of gardens with "trees of knowledge," and of plants, animals, and human lives interwoven by destiny, and yet, it still may be surprising for most to realize that the common houseplant on the window sill can both "make" as well as "hear" sounds emitted by other plants and humans by voice and touch, which now can be analyzed with special instruments. If we could communicate with plants, and if plants had the ability to "think" and then to act accordingly with human beings, could we not, as Christopher Bird suggested in some private conversations we had, discover that the plant kingdom, on which our physical survival depends, also is a complex system that is complementary to our existence?

Korean artist, Nam June Paik, a wiz-engineer, researcher at California Institute of the Arts and inventor of the first video-synthesizer, understood this interconnection. He created a TV Garden Exhibition that was later displayed at the Guggenheim Museum in New York in the year 2000, and also the Tate Museum, 2002 (London), to show how science and nature can come together with music (e.g., Beethoven) and plants. As colleagues, I (J.J.) worked with Paik years ago planning and constructing the music using measuring devices of optical and musical signals on plants. In his exhibition at the Guggenheim, when certain sounds emanated from the TV sets the leaves would rustle on the plants. Paik's design has its home in the Buddhist belief that all things are interdependent and that technology is not necessarily in conflict with nature.

Yet, what if it were possible to hear the plants sing? A well-known device was designed at the spiritual eco-community called the Damanhur Federation in northern Italy, specifically produced by their Devodama Company. It is probably one of the best "commercially available" devices for the purpose of getting plants to sing. It started with research back in the 1970s. One of the early devices was called the U1 device which was based on a variation of the Wheatstone bridge; basically, it transposed electromagnetic impulses of the plants into melodies. By having one fixed resistor and another variable electrode, the device was specifically designed to measure the variations of impedance (electrical resistance) between the fixed and variable electrodes with one being hooked up to the plant and the other placed in the soil.

The engineers at Damanhur understood that variance differences between the two electrode signals allowed them to turn the variations into music. An algorithm was created by the engineers to create specific digital sounds that became notes, and in some cases, melodies, depending on the various signals the device received.

Beyond the specialized language, what this means is that the reactions of plants are not only physical or chemical, but also are created from the current situations around them and sometimes their memories. Damanhur has even found that when leaves are cut on a plant, the plant emits sounds of disturbance.

Esperide Ananas writes in her book *The Music of the Plants: For whom the plants play* about the sound device from Damanhur that has been used now in numerous experiments. In one, she describes that the root of Indian corn (maize) was found to emit a constant ticking at 220 Hz.

Using the equipment from Damanhur, the Music of the Plants®, our Academy For Future Science composer, Anyah Dishon, has performed many concerts with plants in several countries, in auditoriums, schools, and permaculture classes, and at private showings. When in international locations, she works with new plants from that region and donates them after the performance. Thus, at many of our conferences, we have used sound devices like the ones from Damanhur that help us to create beautiful plant music meditations. Anyah, while on stage, is able to work with the plants and engage the audience in singing with the plant music, demonstrating plant intelligence through the Music of the Plants® technology.

She told us: "The plant music brings a feeling of joy, and an experience of the celestial teamwork of many realms working together during the creation of this realm. I developed my musical connection with plants first by communing with the plants without any technology. Then through a synchronicity of events, I began using the Music of the Plants® technology. On my music CDs, I allow the plants to sing but then sometimes I also sing with them. I have three plants at home that I sing with a lot; they are called Leonardo, St. Kateri, and Rigan, and each demonstrates a different plant music style or personality. Leonardo is more classical, St. Kateri has something of a Renaissance feel that heals one's heart, and Rigan reflects a playful jazz dance type with "happy feet" rhythms and notes! I take my Pachira plants with me, if I can, to live concerts for events that promote holistic, healthy ways of environmental stewardship. I love singing with plants and having them sing as it engages the audience while demonstrating plant intelligence."

Anyah has recorded plant music on an album called *Trees of Life*, where we also contribute as singers on other songs. We have been charmed by the plant music we have heard through the devices and have always been impressed by the beautiful vibratory patterns of this music. Music generated by the plants truly reveal the interconnection we all have with sacred sound and the proper sacred attitude to the songs of the soul and the greater creation that sings through all life as a symphony of the Divine.

As social scientists and music researchers, the first time we tried experiments with music and plants many years ago, we learned that it was better to let go of the rational mind and follow the notes produced by the plant as in a simple mantra without trying to lead with our own musical style. Others who have tried to find the harmonic-mathematical-rhythmic logic to the sounds made by the plants have become frustrated. We found that the best approach when composing with them is simply to establish an emotional contact with the plant's environment, bearing in mind that it is a living being very different to the complexities of a human. If we hold the visualization of a whirling blue-green planet as a vehicle for cooperation between the plant and human presences, we follow our intuition and our empathy. When we succeed in doing all this in a powerful moment of chanting, we notice that the plant begins to produce notes and sequences that are different from what came before, or that the notes or songs we are producing are the right thing at the right time. Often, surprising dialogues are created between human being and plant, and everything takes on a different flavor which leaves us with a sense of unusual fulfilment.

Anyah has found that little plants in pots will sing uninterruptedly all day long with clearly noticeable differences in style depending on the time of day and the song in your heart. There are plants that sing whether or not they have contact with human beings at that moment and plants that sound out with more vigor when invited by human beings to do so. But repeatedly, we find that there is a great difference between the sounds produced by plants when they are alone and the sounds they make when human beings approach them with the intention of establishing a relationship, even without necessarily touching them. Roses, for example, respond very well in terms of harmonic variation during emotional contact with people, and will produce more or less repetitive sequences that a human musician can easily tune into.

It is very evident that this musical ability of plants is a reality, as the same plant can sound very different in the morning and at night and very different at different times of the day. Every plant emits a different playful symphony. Some plants seem to be more active in the evening, others in the morning, and every plant emits a different and distinctive orchestration of notes that does not seem to be linked to its size or type.

Our musician associates at Sacred Resonance and The Academy For Future Science, Australia, Darren Curtis and Bradley Pitt, also have created some beautiful plant concerts that have played to sell-out crowds at botanical gardens in South Australia.

Moreover, by using these electronic devices, we can observe how the plants "react" and seem to interact in a precisely positive way with their surroundings including in the midst of audiences. Indeed, plants in the home or a university lab, or out in nature, are capable of master performances of sounds. Some even believe they react to feelings of love and also danger. Also, among the numerous senses already discovered in plants, the possibility that they have something similar to our sense of hearing is becoming more and more accepted.

Reading about these experiments, one can't help reflecting on the implications of the harm major industries are doing when they cut down forests and kill the oldest and most important trees. This brings harm not just to the world but to ourselves and our ability to ever comprehend the greatness of Life.

The very same prejudice that leads us to think there are clear divisions between the kingdoms, and causes us to base our relationship with life and with the plant and animal kingdoms on a hierarchy of values with human beings at the top, prevents us from seeing an overall integrated ecosystem in which each species and each living being—human, bacteria, animal, and plant—has equal importance for the system and should be treated with the same dignity.

Countless tests, many prototypes and re-workings of technology have produced many devices for human-animal-plant communication. I, J.J. Hurtak, worked with music engineers like Morton Subotnik (father of the "first electronic symphony" and the Buchla Synthesizer) who was working on musical devices that emulate the sound of birds and insects, producing music by modifying the electric conductivity.

With this understanding, we need to also include all animals, even the whales and dolphins of the sea. They seem, like plants, to be able to sing, mainly with low-pitched sounds which can be heard some 20 miles away. Their sounds are unique as they simply seem to use whistles or pulsed calls or "clickings." Although we cannot understand them, these sounds are used for social interactions. We now know that mother whales use these signals to locate their children. Recently, it was discovered that cows are also known to make unique sounds, and researchers are studying them more thoroughly in hopes of determining their health and well-being in the midst of a herd. Then there is also echolocation that dolphins seem to use. As scientists have begun to interpret these sounds, they realize that the dolphins are actually "seeing" with the sounds and echoes that they use to identify surrounding objects.

The Indigenous cultures speak of cosmic trees that connect humanity with all life within the universe and show the way for Divine consciousness to descend into matter, and also to ascend to the higher realms of the Divine Nature. Instead of taking these stories as superstitions left over from another age, we might interpret their poetic and metaphorical language in the light of the very recent discoveries of our role as co-evolutionists.

Plants are intelligent; they communicate among themselves and listen to what we are saying. Their emotions and feelings seem to be similar to ours and can be shared when we meet with our living surroundings. To honor our organic neighbors, hug a tree trunk and rest your forehead against its bark, or simply shut your eyes and try to perceive the essence of a little plant you have on your windowsill. In this way, you can become aware that we live amidst self-aware creatures ready to enter into contact with us.

We still have a long way to go before we realize that we are one with the eco-system in which we dwell and before we recognize how much all lives are interwoven with the Trees of Life. Yet, the boldest scientists are showing the way. Maybe, if we listened to the whisper of the plants and trees, our evolution would be more harmonious, happier, and faster.

In conclusion, the experiences in the field of plant music are surely among the most compelling. Plants have given us great insights into the power of bio-music, bio-geometry, and paraphysical communication over a great distance using particular sounds. Legends all over the world, on every continent and in every age, speak of sentient trees, of gardens with trees of knowledge, of plant, human, and Divine lives interwoven by destiny. Rather than being on the lower chain-of-being, plants' "brainlessness" turns out to be their greatest strength, and perhaps the most valuable inspiration we can share with them is a musical conversation.

SOUND AND GEOMETRY

———— ∞ ————

*T*here can be but few who have not seen the beauty of the inspirational images captured in water exposed to harmonious music, thoughts, and environments in the work of Dr. Masaru Emoto from Tokyo, Japan, in his book *The Hidden Messages in Water*. For those few, we will summarize that he placed water taken from different locations in nature and different circumstances in a petri dish at minus 2 degrees centigrade. Some of his water samples were subjected to various sounds, and some to either positive or negative thoughts like "love," "good thoughts," or "hate." Then he looked at the shape of the water and found both beautiful and murky formations. Overall, the water knows a good thing when it is exposed to it!

Dr. Emoto's work and accomplishments, together with that of his colleagues worldwide, are far reaching with data accurate enough to be approved for use in scientific circles studying the paranormal aspects of mind, as well as "sound over matter." He was able to clearly demonstrate that the image of water also changed based on peaceful locations, human generated musical compositions, or positive thoughts, showing a vast complexity of beautiful patterns constructed depending on the variety of circumstances. Ice crystals, at temperatures of -2 or -3 degrees Fahrenheit, after being exposed to positive thoughts or sacred sound environments would form perfect, beautiful, generally hexagonal patterns. The secret, according to Emoto, was positive energy, positive intentions, and the use of positive musical sound patterns based on love-generated signals of creative expression regardless of language and cultural settings.

Emoto's results are sensational, and we had the rare opportunity with our colleague Alan Steinfeld, of inviting him for his first New York lecture, where he spoke before 800 people. Most importantly for our topic here, Emoto and associates tested the effects of various types of music from Eastern music to American classical pieces, from traditional classical compositions of Mozart or Beethoven to other melodic music (e.g., *Madame Butterfly*, John Lennon's *Imagine*), and beautiful coherent shapes of water molecules would develop. However, he also showed how water exposed to heavy metal music and songs such as Elvis Presley's *Heartbreak Hotel* would change and became more chaotic.

His work underscores the reality that we humans are in a body that is approximately 55-75% water, depending on our age. We are continually developing our own internal geometry depending on the positive force field of the water crystals throughout our body.

In our discussions with Emoto in his office lab in Tokyo (2011), he acknowledged the basic significance of his work and confirmed the proof of a living flow pattern connected also with sound waves that can quickly assemble living and non-living matter into visible expression. In effect, under certain conditions, chaos becomes order, dissipation becomes re-integration and structure in a new form, and negative thoughts become uncomely and ugly patterns whereas positive thoughts, and, most remarkably, beautiful music, translates into beautiful vibratory expressions of consciousness in a water medium that is the "hidden message."

This brings us to the great work of Hans Jenny (1904-1972), a Swiss physician and research scientist, who in his later years, as a follower of the school known as Anthroposophy, developed his personal passion, taking sound vibrations and showing how various frequencies naturally create specific geometries, allowing sound not only to be heard, but also seen. He found out that changing the frequency changes the shape and he called his technique Cymatics.

Jenny was not the first to demonstrate this. In the late 1600s, Robert Hooke was able to create nodal patterns associated with various modes of vibration of glass plates using household flour. German physicist and musician, Ernst Florens Friedrich Chladni (1756-1827), about 100 years after Hooke, used similar techniques. He took powder, placed it on metal plates and played the violin close enough to the plates for the bow sound to create a visual effect. The vibrations of the violin's bow made the powder move from nodes to antinodes creating some amazing shapes and sometimes building up from antinodes to nodes. Nodes are locations which are stationary with zero amplitude and no real movement. Antinodes are locations at maximum amplitude where movement is seen. The nodes are said to appear, thus, in low pressure regions while the antinodes form at high pressure regions.

Jenny, because of the times, was able to do much more. Being a physician, he also used this technique to work with hard of hearing and mute individuals so that if they spoke a letter, they could see it forming. He configured primitive amplifiers and constructed frequency generators. He also used crystals which worked as transducers. Jenny became famous for taking glass plates and covering their surfaces in flour and then having a violin with a rosin bow played across the edge of the glass. Later, he moved from flour to sand, metal filings and even dust, and, yes, "sacred tonal geometries" formed from a variety of vibrational frequencies. He also later exchanged the sand for liquids, and he also used "Chladni's Lycopodium" powder (spores of the club moss) and much more.

Through Jenny's sound geometry apparatus, he converted frequencies as vibrations to create a visual resonance on steel plates and documented his results in books and on film as he experimented with changing tones using various sound frequencies and amplitudes.[3]

Specifically, Jenny made use of crystal oscillators attached to metal plates often with vibrating membranes. He placed quartz sand, flour, or other materials like iron filings onto a metal plate, generally 1 mm thick, while the width of the plate would be varied from that of an eardrum to greater. Basically, Jenny created what was known already as a "tonoscope" where the spoken sound or musical note could be sung, which gave him the ability through precise sound generation to create various geometries. "Tonoscopes" had been around for a while in Jenny's time but he moved their use into an entirely new scenario.

Overall, he found that the lower tones created simple yet distinct pictures, while higher tones created more complicated structures. Perhaps most controversial is the complicated Sri Yantra from the Hindu and Buddhist traditions which some claim to have seen using similar cymatic frequencies. Jenny saw this all as the "triadic nature" of vibration where you can hear the sound, observe the pattern, as well as sense the vibration.

Darren Curtis tells us: "At Sacred Resonance, we have been exploring through the arts and in our personal experiments, the science of cymatics. The images we have created via sound waves are resonating with vibrating water which then transforms into a variety of geometric shapes. Our goal is to visualize how sound can affect water, as our bodies are 60 plus percent water. So instead of using sand or metal filings like Hans Jenny, we used water which has the same effect—we think even better. We worked with a variety of sound frequencies, but also worked with ancient sounds that we sang. Our research confirmed what was told in the ancient Sanskrit tradition that the "mantra" as the sound could create various sacred geometries; thus, we have found in our experiments certain sacred sounds and music can create amazing complex sacred geometry patterns using water. Most importantly, sound is form, and form is sound. Once we know that, we know that all life is composed of sacred geometries."

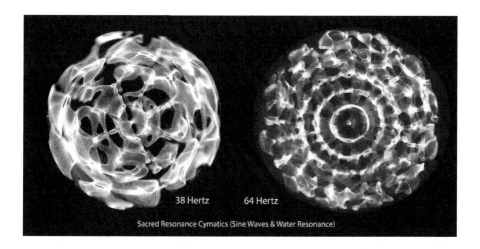

38 Hertz   64 Hertz

Sacred Resonance Cymatics (Sine Waves & Water Resonance)

Darren told us he loves to create these complex beautiful patterns to show how sound and resonance affect our body, mind, and spirit. Thus, he feels this is a new "frequency medicine" where we can transform the dissonance of our body into patterns of coherence, harmony, and perfection.

Others who have followed Jenny's research include our associate John Stuart Reid from the United Kingdom, who has created a CymaScope which is used for analyzing cells within the body based on the water of the cells and their geometry. In working with the CymaScope, Reid hopes to help determine if the geometries that cells reveal, even in "real time" during surgical procedures, would indicate whether they are healthy or cancerous.

Sound cymatics brings us one step closer to seeing how our body is part of the cosmic chorus, and how it is up to us to harmonize it with our mind and soul. In addition to geometry, some theoreticians have also attempted to correlate sound to color. Although there is no specific law that tells you specifically what color to use, consider the following: red is the color of fire, the beginning of the color spectrum. It is the primal color of nature and the rainbow, the color of blood. Red is primal matter, and if we take the wavelength given off by the red spectrum, calculate the frequencies and transpose the frequency down from 10^{14} to between 10^1 to 10^2 cps (cycles per second = Hertz) by divisions of 2, we find that A is at 55 Hz which is the fundamental tone or the primal tone of nature.

Many creative geniuses throughout the centuries, including Isaac Newton in the 18th century and I.J. Belmont, a 20th century NY artist interested in "Color Music Expressions," have each created their own chromesthesia, that is, correlations between sound and color. Almost each person has created their own chart with, for example, the musical note "A" designating colors that range from green to blue or violet. Helmholtz wrote in his book entitled *The Sensations of Tone* of the correlations between color-sound equivalences by stating that the tenor C relates to yellow. Therefore, Helmholtz actually considered: G = ultra violet, F# & F = violet, E = indigo blue, D# = cyanogen blue, D = greenish blue, C# = green, C = yellow, B = orange, A# = orange red, A, G# and G = red, F# = infrared, and we agree. The name "Adam" (the first man) means "red" in Hebrew which may relate to the first sound that the natural spectrum used in its unfoldment from the higher manifestations. It was the first sound of the first hydrogen explosion, the so-called Big Bang of scientific evolution.

We, too, are matter composed of particles; thus, we, too, have the ability to receive the energy from sound and ultimately become as waves of Light.

THE MUSIC OF THE SPHERES

*M*any years ago, the great Hellenistic writer, Heraclitus, spoke of the "Music of the Spheres," the music of how space is a symphony of creation.

We just learned how music relates to geometry, but how does it relate to the planets and stars? We need to first compare light to sound. Every time you see light, you are seeing waves of electromagnetic energy traveling towards or around you. If in a vacuum, light would be traveling at 186,282 miles/sec, (299,792.458 km/sec), the speed of light (c). However, some waves are in the visible spectrum, and visible light ranges from violet at 4000 Angstroms (400 nanometers) to dark red at 7000 Angstroms (700 nanometers). Sound waves, which are mechanical pressure waves passing through the air, are much slower than light waves and travel only about 767 miles/hour (343 meters/ sec), compared to the speed of light which is 670,616,629 miles/hour ($3\text{x}10^{10}$ meters/sec).

As previously mentioned, sound and light do coordinate as there is a correlation between wavelength (light) and frequency (light and/or sound). This can be seen in the following equation: $\lambda = c/f$ where "λ" (lambda) stands for wavelength in meters, "c" is the speed of light, and "f" is the frequency, in this case the frequency of light. This same formula works, however, for sound—if "*c*" relates to the speed of sound in meters per second, then "*f*" relates to the frequency of sound. Regardless, the higher the activated frequency, the shorter the wavelength. Because all waves move at the same speed (*c*), the number of wave peaks passing by a given point in one second depends on the wavelength. That number of passing peaks is known as "frequency."

A sound wave of 100 Hz means that it is vibrating 100 times per second, or that 100 wave peaks pass a given point in a second's duration. A sound of 500 Hz is vibrating 500 times per second. This means that the wavelength (the measurement of the length of the wave) correlates inversely with the Hertz number (frequency). In other words, the shorter the wavelength, the higher the frequency or Hz, or the higher the pitch of a sound, the shorter the wavelength.

Johannes Kepler, as revealed in his 1619 book entitled *Harmonices Mundi* (*The Harmony of the World*), empirically studied the path of our local planets as well as Earth, attempting to find a relationship between the motions of the planets and Ptolemy's musical system (2nd century AD) written about in his treatise entitled *Harmonikon* (or *Harmonics*).

Kepler (1571-1630), an astronomer, lived just after the era of Copernicus (1473-1543), and during the time of Galileo (1564-1642) who already used his telescope to determine the movement of planets orbiting around the sun. He did emerge at a perfect time, as Copernicus had just initiated a move away from an earth-centered model of belief, and with the help of Galileo, a contemporary of Kepler, the thought of the day was moving to a heliocentric model. So, by the time Kepler wrote about the Music of the Spheres, *Musica Universalis*, it was mainly accepted that the sun was the center of our system, and that planets orbited around it.

Using the angular speeds of each planet at their aphelion (farthest point from the sun) and their perihelion (closest point to the sun) to produce consonant ratios, Kepler found that the planets were able to form four harmonious chords to which he assigned usually one or two notes to each.

Therefore, Kepler further suggested that the planets of the solar system produced tones as they orbited the sun and, hence, associated a frequency to each planet. All of the mathematics was based on Kepler's Third Law[4] which states that the squares of the orbital periods of the planets are directly proportional to the cubes of the semi-major axes of their orbits. That is ($T1/T2)^2 = (a1/a2)^3$. That may be hard to understand, but what Kepler is saying implies that the period in which a planet orbits the Sun increases rapidly with the radius of its orbit. In other words, a planet closer to the sun is orbiting faster than those farther away.

To Kepler, the universe was a cosmic orchestra. He viewed all the planets as if they were singing in a celestial choir. Thus, he ascribed various musical notes to the planets depending on their positions with regard to the sun and their rotations. Kepler took the fast orbit of the planet Mercury, which is about 88 days, and gave it various tones depending on its various positions relative to its orbital speed. So, for example, in his chart translated from the Latin in his Book 5, Chapter 7 called *Harmonias Universales Omnium*, he has charts on the "Harmonies of all the Planets, or Universal Harmonies in the Minor Mode" where he tries to put two different relationships (b and c) in concord with the following notes:

at one position Mercury was an E ♭ 7, B ♭ 7 and G6
but then it would change to E ♭ 7, C7 and G6, and so on ...

Venus was E ♭ 6 and E ♭ 5
but then it would change to E ♭ 6, C6 and E ♭ 5 ...

Earth was G4 to B ♭ 4
and Earth would change to just G4 ...

Mars was G3 – this stayed the same in one position
but might also change ...

Jupiter was B♭1
but this would change to C1 ...

Saturn was B♭0 and G0
and would change to just G0, and so on ...

So, this was only one of many relations he saw with the Music of the Spheres as it was all based on movement. He went many steps further, as well, calculating Saturn's maximum and minimum angular speeds which he felt were a 4:5 ratio, relating to a major third, while Jupiter was a 5:6 ratio, or minor third. Mars was 2:3, Earth was 15:16, and Venus was 24:25.

Interestingly, Kepler clearly considered Mercury as a soprano, Venus and Earth as the altos, Mars as a tenor, and the biggest and slower planets, Jupiter and Saturn, as the bass or baritones, a veritable heavenly symphony!

In all of this, Kepler saw evidence that a Divine Mind existed behind the universe. His fundamental belief, as for many of his era, was that geometry "provided the Creator with the model for decorating the whole world," and it was Kepler's wish to find those proportions in musical terms, much like Ptolemy in *Harmonikon*.

In effect, human life was seen as part of a larger natural cosmophysical micro-symphony capable of awareness via larger vibratory signal ranges in receiving and using the sequences of sounds and vibrations for comprehending our living "eco-system." Recent Russian researchers A. Trofimov and V. Kaznacheev have also pointed to the close interrelationship of paraphysical energies between our planet, the solar system, and the immediate universe that affect the human body in their book, *Reflections on Life and Intelligence on Planet Earth*.

Kepler was clearly a pioneer but he did have a rival, Robert Fludd, who simultaneously was trying to determine the harmonic theory of the universe. Now we know, with the perspective of hindsight, that Kepler won out, as NASA developed the Kepler Space Telescope which functioned from 2009-2018. One of its main missions was to look for exoplanets in space but it also analyzed various stars by means of sound vibrations.

Of course, years before that there were the Voyager 1 and 2 Spacecraft (both launched in 1977) which carried onboard the Voyager Golden Record labeled *The Sounds of Earth*. The content of the record was determined by a committee whose head was none other than Carl Sagan. The Golden Record (really 2 golden phonographs) contains sounds of animals and nature including bird and whale sounds (*Songs of the Humpback Whale* by Roger Payne), 55 ancient and modern languages, speeches as well as music from Bach, Mozart, Stravinsky, folk songs, and more modern songs like Chuck Berry's *Johnny B. Goode* and more—all were added to a type of Gold LP, specifically two gold-anodized aluminum plaques, which are still traveling and are now beyond our solar system, traveling in what is officially classified as "interstellar" space.

Yet, what about listening to the stars? Studying the sound of stars for our space program begins with oscillations. We have been studying our sun's vibrations known as the study of helioseismology since the early 1960s but it was not until the French-led Convection, Rotation, and Planetary Transits (COROT) space telescope, launched in 2006, that we began to listen to hundreds of stars at a time. By now, the sound-wave data is coming in like an avalanche. It started with COROT, then moved to the Kepler Space Telescope, which had a 0.95-metre-aperture telescope—nine times the sensitivity of COROT's, and now it is with TESS (Transiting Exoplanet Survey Satellite), Hubble, and even the James Webb Space Telescope.

When we examine and record the oscillations of stars, it is called "asteroseismology," and that was exactly what the Kepler Space Telescope was able to do. Just as Kepler said, the oscillations of the sound waves which tend to bounce around inside the stars reveal to us their age, size, and more. They literally hum to us.

So, Kepler did it again, as before the Kepler Space Telescope only about 20 stars had been measured. Kepler confirmed that the universe is not silent, but part of a cosmic orchestra. We just cannot hear it. Now the infrasound acoustic waves are being received by telescopes, and just as Kepler said, the biggest stars are like the bass or baritones. Elizabeth Landau of NASA's Exoplanet Exploration Program agrees with aspects of Kepler's explanation that "the stars in the sky are performing a concert, one that never stops." Yes, the deepest sounds, like tubas and double basses, come from the larger stars while the smaller ones are more high-pitched like flutes. Of course, it isn't just a single note but an orchestration of notes.

William Chaplin, an astrophysicist at the University of Birmingham, UK, and a specialist in asteroseismology, with his colleagues published their analysis of acoustic oscillations observed by Kepler in 500 Sun-like stars back in 2011. It's not too different from the European composer Gustav Holst's orchestral suite, *The Planets*, and now NASA is traveling across the country with Holst's music combined with their images. Planetary music is real, and even though Holst created a mere musical abstraction without any basis in real science, the resonance patterns directly connect with the evolution of the universe. However, now there is music we can listen to that the planets themselves have composed such as the sounds received from NASA's Cassini spacecraft, as it approached Jupiter.

When Cassini made its fly-bys of the planets, it recorded a 50-second track of screeches and bleeps as it went by the moon of Jupiter called Ganymede, (e.g., June 7, 2021). The Juno Mission collected much of the data as it flew through the moon's magnetosphere. Similarly, the "Waves" instrument onboard the unmanned Juno spacecraft sent to analyze Jupiter's magnetosphere, is now reinterpreting as "music," Ganymede's magnetic and electric emissions. Shifting the sounds into the audible, you can hear it sing as the "Waves" instrument picks up the electric and magnetic radio waves, now turned into audio sounds.

Before that, Voyager recorded waves in the gas of charged particles as low radio frequencies and sent them back to Earth where scientists converted the oscillations of the changing electromagnetic fields detected by the space craft magnetometers into sound waves to bring us the electromagnetic voices from our solar system. These have now been converted to sound waves in our audible range, and NASA commissioned a musical work based on radio waves gathered from the entire solar system by the Voyager, Galileo, and Cassini to create the *First Symphony of the Planets.*

This might all be wonderful, but the field is developing rapidly, as in 2018, NASA's InSight Mars lander recorded the sound of winds on Mars. These are the first real sounds ever recorded from another planet.

So, Johannes Kepler was not that far off. NASA agrees that even the stars are performing a concert. We can't hear them because there is no way for any audible sounds to travel any significant distance, but the electromagnetic (and sometimes ion-acoustic) waves are present for us to record and convert.

The asteroseismology studies have now clearly moved past the Kepler Space Telescope with the 2018 launch of TESS (NASA's Transiting Exoplanet Survey Satellite) which took over where the Kepler Space Telescope left off, looking at the sound waves of many of the red giants in our universe to detect stellar vibrations and even the "hum" of the universe.

Also of interest is that NASA has made public a recording of strange "sounds" that astronauts reported hearing in 1969 while on the far side of the Moon, while they were out of radio contact with the Earth. The story behind these unusual whistling noises was shown on the cable channel *Discovery*, as part of a series called *NASA's Unexplained Files*. Specifically, during the Apollo 10 mission (May 1969), the astronauts were able to circle the backside of the Moon. This happened before the first astronauts even set foot on the moon in July that same year. The three astronauts on board were Thomas Stafford, John Young, and Eugene Cernan. The transcript was released in 2008, some 40 years later by NASA, and the actual recording of the sounds some 7 years later. The strange sounds lasted about an hour. They were also transmitted to Houston mission control. In the transcript to NASA, one hears:

Cernan: Whoooooooooooo.

Young: Did you hear that whistling sound, too?

Cernan: Yeah. Sounds like—you know, outer-space-type music.

Young: I wonder what it is?

It now has been claimed that the sounds were simply interference caused by radios that were close to each other in the lunar module and the command module. Yet, strangely, they were only heard on the backside of the moon and for a long period of time.

Another key "outer space" project involved with sound-signals is SETI (the Search for Extraterrestrial Intelligence). The idea of SETI is not new; it has been around for a long time. In fact, as early as 1896, Nikola Tesla suggested we could use a wireless transmitter to contact beings living on Mars, and in 1899, he thought he might have done that with his own equipment.

Then, in 1960, Frank Drake from Cornell University started Project Ozma using a 26-meter (85-foot) radio telescope from Green Bank, West Virginia. Later, in 1980, Carl Sagan with associates continued the push forward going to Oak Ridge Observatory (Harvard, Massachusetts). Their projects went through various transformations from "Meta" to "Beta," then finally NASA began to help fund the MOP (Microwave Observing Project). Now the "search for extraterrestrial life" through observation of signals from outer space is being carried out all over the world from many different telescopes, including the Green Bank Telescope.

In 2015, "Breakthrough Listen" was created which, in 2019, teamed up with the TESS team to look for signs of ET life. SETI is now funded mainly by private contributions. In recent years, they have called our attention to unusual signals that have been received, such as from our nearest stellar cluster—the Centauri constellation. Although, as of the writing of this book, no confirmation of "intelligent signals" from outer space have been accepted as valid; nonetheless, there have been many unusual signals from stars connected with Arcturus and Proxima Centauri, both areas that have also been cited by UFOlogists as having signs of life.

A final thought generated by the genius of Kepler is that if all life is vibrations, we too may be part of the vibrations. This brings us to String theory as the possible theory of everything. Although the theory may not be a perfect theory of everything, it does posit that vibrations do not originate within us but within the entirety of the universe, including the fact that we may be connected with higher dimensions. We live in the 3rd dimension, and the 4th dimension is time, but there is also the 5th to the 12th dimension, where similar forms exist as light energy. Everything is vibrating, and we are part of that vast orchestration. So, all aspects of life in the universe convey the picture that we are truly cosmo-planetary-ecological beings working within a vast vibratory system of life, here and beyond.

SOUND WAVES AND SPIRIT

*W*hen we hear sounds, especially music, various parts of our brain become activated. For example, the amygdala reacts emotionally to music. The hippocampus helps us to remember music. The auditory cortex helps us recognize the music and its various tones and to respond very quickly to threatening sounds. Other parts of our brain are for movement such as dance, clapping, or tapping our feet. What is taking place is that acoustic sensations are passing through complex neural pathways to these centers that process acoustic stimuli in the cerebral cortex.

We know that sound is a wave created by vibrating objects (air pressure). For example, vibrations in the vocal cords cause the air to vibrate, creating sound waves. When we hear music, the vibrations passing through our ears are decoded and reconstructed in the ears, first through the spiral structure, the cochlea, which has a golden or Fibonacci spiral as its shape. Low frequency sounds are received by the inner spiral of the cochlea and the high frequency ones by the outer portion of the spiral. The very structure of this organ alone should indicate to each of us that we did not evolve from happenstance or Darwinistic evolution, but from a spiral geometry which comes from a higher coding of Light-light. The hair cells in the ear region and the cochlea translate the sound vibrations into electrical signals that are then processed in various parts of the brain, especially through the neurons. So, inside the brain, a sound bio-geometric pattern is created that resounds with each audible frequency.

Some fifty years ago, the creative art and film genius, Walt Disney, gathered a group of leading scientists and musicologists to form the faculty at California Institute of the Arts in Valencia, California. At that time, I (J.J. Hurtak) was one of the founding faculty, a social scientist, composer, and futurist who taught classes in the School of Critical Studies and also the School of Music. Included on the faculty were the famous Leonard Bernstein, Andre Previn, and Ravi Shankar. Desiree also took classes in both the Music and the Design Schools. With other faculty members, we worked to answer some intriguing questions about music and its connection with the patterns of human consciousness. Within the music labs of Cal Arts, we set out to examine the frontiers of music through biofeedback for relieving stress and to determine how to simply relax.

Biofeedback became known as a way to train the human mind to be highly sensitive and creative; to relieve stress and quiet the mind. This can be done through certain breathing techniques, but it also can be done through sound. Biofeedback is where the body is hooked up to electrical sensors that give you a reading of your heart rate (ECG) so you can better understand your body processes. Some more advanced systems even have an electroencephalograph (EEG) so you can read your brain waves when you are doing certain things like listening to music, for example. Then this feedback helps you understand and make subtle changes in your body. The purpose of biofeedback is for users to adjust their emotions based on the feedback. The EEG data as well as the ECG in "real time" helps the analysis of the emotional state of the body and the mind. This feedback helps you understand your body's reactions while listening to music and how to calm your reactions to your environment.

At that time in the early 1970s, leading musicians in California were experimenting with music designed for biofeedback, which is adapted from the combination of musical and emotional orchestrations that were fed electronically into the mental control of the human sensory system.

Serious studies had already begun in the late 1960s and early 1970s with American scientist Dr. Joe Kamiya (University of Chicago), Russian scientists like Edward Naumov (Department for Technical Parapsychology, Moscow), and Czech scientist, Dr. Milan Ryzl (pioneer in parapsychology from Prague), who all seemed, through their independent research, to discover the importance of biofeedback.

In the early 1970s, the embryonic discipline of biofeedback centered around the simple training of using muscular galvanic responses to evoke signals. It has since been carefully expanded to cover a plethora of fields. Since that time, the studies from the Indian Swami Rama at the Academy of Parapsychology and Medicine in Los Altos, California, the research of Dr. William Tiller at Stanford University, and the work of Elmer and Alice Green at the Menninger Clinic in Topeka, Kansas, allowed the discipline to grow as it became an integral part of what can be called the science of Parapsychology and Medicine.

Working with music and biofeedback led to the discovery of how unique musical patterns and sound frequencies can move the mind into different states of consciousness. For the most part, the brain produces frequencies defined as gamma, beta, alpha, theta, and delta waves. They can be defined as follows:

Delta waves: 0.4-3.9 Hz for states of deep sleep, coma

Theta waves: 3.9-7.5 Hz for dreams and deeper awareness

Alpha waves: 7.5-13 Hz for meditation and contemplative awareness

Beta waves: 13-30 Hz for mental activity and perception

Gamma waves: 30-100+ Hz for cognition and peak concentration

Although gamma waves are on the higher end of the spectrum, Tibetan Buddhist meditators tested in their meditative states were said to be able to operate on this frequency, that is with peak concentration. Specifically, long-term meditators have been shown to be able to self-induce high-amplitude gamma synchrony during mental practice. In fact, according to Dr. Lee Bartel, who is a professor of Music at the University of Toronto, the frequency at which neurons are likely to connect is in the range of about 40 Hz.

It is important to realize that all these brain wave frequencies exist within the brain, but there is one frequency range that becomes the dominant frequency while the others move more into the background. I (J.J. Hurtak) also taught classes at California Institute of the Arts on how to use biofeedback training to take people into enhanced alpha wave frequencies needed to bring them into deeper contemplation, as well as higher states of awareness. Much of this work was also systematically studied by Dr. Stanley Krippner in the United States and Dr. Vail Kaznacheev of the Russian Academy of Sciences in Novosibirsk.

Although our brain can operate on many frequency wavelengths, the alpha wave frequencies calm us, providing a deeper, higher state of meditation that leads to guidance from the Creative Mind. The gamma waves provide the focus to accomplish our mission in life. However, it is important to add that beta (waking) and delta (deep sleep) states are also important. In fact, all frequencies in their own unique way can allow us to receive insights and experiences based upon higher levels of information perhaps from our spirit guides or a Higher Intelligence who wish to teach us in our waking state or even in our dreams (theta state). Thus, under special conditions with biofeedback and sound, the human mind could reach higher states of consciousness in which human learning and the acquisition of knowledge could be accelerated.

Yes, normal music can also entrain our minds. Music therapy has been used on everyone from coma patients to psychiatric patients with some surprisingly powerful results. That may be because our brain is so receptive to sound. In fact, an annoying sound can keep us awake all night. Today, there is what is known as the "Alive Inside" organization which provides headphones and music, mainly popular music of the person's era, to elderly patients with dementia and Alzheimer's as a way to bring them back to a better level of cognition.

There is also the "Mozart Effect," based on studies of Wolfgang Amadeus Mozart's Sonata in D Major for Two Pianos K448. The major promotor of this is music visionary Don Campbell whose studies sought to enhance IQ. A professor at the University of California (Irvine), he and fellow colleagues believe that listening to Mozart's music, and similar classical music from Bach and others, for ten minutes a day can improve your performance on spatial-reasoning tasks given immediately after the listening sessions. This was taken so seriously that in 1998, the then Governor of Georgia, Zell Miller, ensured that all babies born in a hospital went home with a copy of Mozart, Bach, and others to help them connect their trillions of brain cells. Although this lasted only a short time, and most people no longer consider the "Mozart Effect" to be a way to enhance IQ, there are studies that show that it has helped with epilepsy, as there is accumulated evidence that classical music stimulates the brain's EEG activity to produce balanced frequency spectrums.

It is now clear that higher states of human consciousness can mobilize biofeedback signals in all parts of the body to send and receive signals from both local areas of testing and non-local areas in any part of the globe. We are discovering our human capacity as biotransducers, vehicles for using multiple energy fields that range from the bio-music of the cell to the expanded quantum mind that encircles the earth. Breathtaking discoveries are showing the true interconnection of bio-transmission systems and communication channels on all sound-vibratory levels of the body.

The acoustical and music networks in the human "Body Electric" are, in fact, a type of living "light ware" of the inner mind-body that makes vital and micro sound vibrations that connect mind-to-mind and mind-to-body even over great "non-local areas." The good news is we are becoming more aware through science, even in the field of quantum mechanics, that life works through entanglement as a type of matrix, having some aspect of nonlocal awareness. Acoustic signals serve to connect the human being with the perceived energy patterns of the global brain and remind us that "the human body is the temple of sound" and "[the] place to experience the Divine Music of the Spheres."

While our ears cannot hear sounds below 20 Hz, it is possible to feed lower frequencies into the brain through a special kind of music. Some of the best work in the field of combining sound and consciousness awareness was done by the late Robert Monroe, who began a sonic exploration mainly to create spontaneous out-of-body-experiences (OBE). Monroe pioneered a neuroscience revolution that has produced a variety of acoustic techniques for enhancing human consciousness and performance. Specifically, scientists at the Monroe Institute (Virginia) began work with the use of "binaural beats." Using his engineering background, Monroe applied the binaural beats and developed a program of binaural stimulation to expand human conscious awareness to create a gateway to higher consciousness. We have also used binaural beats in our seminars to demonstrate that the brain can receive these lower frequencies and augment consciousness.

What are binaural beats? They were first discovered by Heinrich Wilhelm Dove in 1839. Binaural beats are created inside the brain by the arithmetic processing of two separate frequencies. You must use a headset to get the full effect. For example, when one ear hears 428 Hz and the other ear 438 Hz, you will hear 10 Hz as a result. It is best to use two sounds where the difference is not more than 30 Hz. This is most noticeable under conditions where the two frequencies are separated to stimulate the separate ears, as in a stereo headset. They are considered to be auditory illusions that your brain makes when it hears the two different sound frequencies.

Monroe determined that the entire brain resonates with brain waveform coherence. Although the main purpose was to create Out of Body Experiences, Monroe also was able to balance emotions, increase creativity, increase learning ability and memory, and reduce stress through his biofeedback techniques. The subjective effect of listening to binaural beats can be relaxing or stimulating, depending on the binaural beat frequencies utilized.

There does not seem to be any negative effects from binaural beats, and depending on the "inner beat," they do help people with attention (beta waves) and reducing anxiety (alpha waves) —pretty much anything that the various frequencies (alpha, beta, theta ...) are known to establish. So, if the difference between the beats is 7.5-13 Hz, it seems to enhance the alpha waves in your brain. The amazing thing is—it may not matter if we are listening while awake or asleep. One might think that we don't listen to things while we sleep but that is proving to be untrue. We do listen while we are sleeping!

Within the alpha and theta states of consciousness, we may find higher states of consciousness experience which can alter our state of being. The brain clearly can map colors, geometries, and musical patterns, and together, they operate like a music conductor in organizing trillions of data forms into a highly synchronized "axiatonal" system to align the body to the "nonlocal Consciousness Field" that can point us in the direction of reaching out to greater consciousness dimensions. Monroe, and those who continue this field, developed acoustic patterns that produce dramatic changes in brain wave activity.

Yet, it is not enough to be a passive listener, or to rely on any of the subsequent variations of consciousness expanding audio programs. It is time for us to take off the "headphones" (and pacifier) of our personal transformational process and join together in a collective transformational process, creating harmony where there is chaos.

There are also "isochronic tones" when a single tone is turned on and off rapidly like a pulse. They are usually created at evenly spaced intervals, but can be made to create sharp, distinctive pulses of sound that can become rhythmic to the brain. The single tone can be used alongside monaural beats and binaural beats in a process called brainwave entrainment or "frequency following" response. They can help people to relieve stress and have also been found effective for those with ADHD (attention-deficit hyperactivity disorder).

One can even create a music piece with them either within or exclusively of those tones. We have used isochronic tones in our public lectures with the knowledge of our audience as we believe they can musically reorientate the faculties of the mind to new levels of holistic innovation.

One cannot write a chapter on frequencies and sound without discussing the tuning of instruments. In the 20th century, to create a beautiful instrumental symphony, each musician had to start with a central tuning, which today is 440 Hz for the agreed upon note of "A" (or "LA" in the European based solfege system). However, in ancient times, the Pythagorean tuning was 432 Hz (as "A"). Many New Age musicians argue that the 432 Hz, which is closer to natural sounds, is more resonant not only to our ears but also our body. Alan Howarth told us: "Referring to the western musical note standardized as A = 440 Hz, it can be adjusted to frequencies of the golden mean, resulting in the note A = 432 Hz, which resonates with all of natural design, and is acoustically found in the songs of whales, dolphins, and birds, and our database acoustic standing waves of the architecture of the ancients." Alan believes the note A ranges from 424 Hz to 432 Hz.

Other New Age musicians also use 528 Hz for the "C" which some believe is also stress-reducing, especially affecting the endocrine system and the autonomic nervous system, and is seen as a single note that has some healing powers. According to Leonard Horowitz, it is the Love vibration and works as "medicinal music." Kaho Akimoto, *et.al.* showed at 528 Hz that cortisol significantly decreased, chromogranin A decreased, and oxytocin significantly increased.[5]

In addition, Alan Howarth points out that it is interesting that the ratios of PHI and PI, which are identified as irrational numbers, which could also be described as "infinite numbers," or simply numbers that are part of the Divine infinite of creation, are the foundations of the acoustic frequencies that were revealed in all the ancient structures' measurements. Howarth has also pointed out the importance of one additional infinite number, "e," which is a particular constant known as the Euler number (2.718...). It is fascinating that the formula of PI (3.1415) divided by PHI (1.618) equals 1.9416, then multiplied by the "e" number (2.718) gives us 5.28. Augmenting that by 100 (5.28 X 100) and we arrive at 528 which is the Hz frequency for love and healing.

Perhaps the oldest evidence of music in society can be traced back 7,000 – 9,000 years at Jiahu, China, where archeological excavations as described in *Nature* magazine (1999) revealed several flutes from the Neolithic Age made of bone.[6] In all, six flutes were found amidst the rubble of perhaps many more. The flutes have from 5 to 8 holes and vary in length. The discovery of these complete, playable, multi-note flutes provides a unique opportunity to hear and analyze actual musical sounds produced nine millennia ago. The Chinese team who studied the sounds found they could not use the modern standard of A4 = 440 Hz, but instead had to adopt an arbitrary standard of a much higher frequency where hole 1 = A6 (~ 1760 Hz) and hole 2 = F#6 (~ 1480 Hz) and hole 5 = C6 (~ 1050 Hz).

Now, there are waves that cannot be heard or felt (as in heat), yet which can still affect our bodies. It is through this that we can understand the healing power of waves when the proper resonant vibrations are created.

Although we don't hear it—one of the most natural sounds on the Earth is the Schumann Resonance. Discovered in the early 1950s by Winfried Otto Schumann, it is basically the sounds of the earth's negative polarization and the ionosphere's positive polarization which when lightning strikes in the area creates a field in the order of 7.4 – 8 Hz. It also puts out harmonics above those frequencies as well, but that is the main resonance field, so the normal operating frequency created of the Schumann Resonance is around 7.8 Hz. The harmonic frequencies of 7.8 Hz that is the doubling or tripling of the root frequency sometimes are also present as: 14.1, 20.3, 26, 32.5, 39, and 45 Hz (some researchers have different specific numbers). The higher ranges of 14 – 45 Hz are beta and gamma frequencies.

Thus, the Earth also emits its own sounds, and some come through lightning striking the Earth, which is said to be striking somewhere on Earth at every moment. Strikes have been calculated to be as many as 100 per second. As lightning strikes the Earth, it reverberates off the ionosphere creating ELF (Extremely Low Frequency) signals around the planet. Specifically, the Schumann Resonance is created by quasi standing, electromagnetic waves that exist and are created between the Earth and the lower portions of the ionosphere, where a resonant cavity is created for electromagnetic waves by lightning strikes in the region. That is, the frequency of the Schumann Resonance is dependent upon the size of the cavity between the Earth and the beginning layers of the ionosphere. If the size changes, the frequency changes.

Anything that changes the size of the Earth-ionosphere cavity will alter the frequencies as they simply are vibrating in conjunction with the space of the atmosphere, ionosphere, and magnetosphere surrounding the Earth. These are sub-audible frequencies (generally below 24 Hz) and, thus, closer to the alpha range that again cannot be heard by the ear, but if they could, they would sound strange. They can be detected, however, through tactile input from low-frequency sounds. These low frequency inputs correspond to the frequency spectrum of the bioelectrical activity of the brain. And not just our brains, but also our bodies are sensitized to frequencies and sound wave vibrations that are ultimately harmonized with the Earth and higher planes of spiritual experience. Interestingly enough, the 7.8 Hz is also the alpha frequency of our brain, which means that the earth itself is generating a field to make us calmer and more meditative if we can receive it. Although the very presence, observationally, of the Schumann Resonance does not influence our thoughts, it does play a significant role in our brain's harmony and our ability to create a peaceful environment within ourselves.

HEALING AND SOUND

───── ∞ ─────

*L*ike the stars and planets, all energy in atoms and molecules that make up our body is electromagnetic in nature; it produces electromagnetic fields (EMFs). We have already seen how plants can communicate through this process and how stars make sound. We, too, especially our brains, are not just chemical networks, but electrical networks processing information, constantly allowing for a complex exchange of information in our body.

Royal Raymond Rife (1888 – 1971) understood this early on and was able to use frequencies in the radio frequency range (20 kHz – 300 kHz) to help heal the body. Rife understood that our bodies are, in effect, a large collection of bio-antennae for various frequencies and that, with the right frequencies, bacteria and viruses could be destroyed, and we could be renewed and regenerated. In short, every part of the human body, every DNA strand, all our components modulate electromagnetic waves which are, in essence, the sounds of our cells. We have within us a built-in set of micro-composers for physical and soul evolution.

It is true that "all life is vibration," and this has been physically demonstrated by Evelyn Glennie, who is a deaf percussionist. She cannot hear through her ears but feels low sounds in her legs and feet. The higher notes she typically experiences in particular places on her face, neck, and chest, and thus, she performs some amazing concerts in public. Besides our human brain waves (alpha, beta, theta, delta, gamma), all human cells act like neurons, sending and receiving "sound-related" signals.

We assert that our genetic process is especially influenced by our thoughts, our "bio-consciousness" field, and also by sound vibrations. We wrote about this with Russian scientist Peter Gariaev, in a discussion of *Key 202* from my (J.J.'s) book entitled *The Book of Knowledge: The Keys of Enoch*® which aligns with Gariaev's own study of Linguistic-Wave Genetics (LWG). This book shows how the coding of DNA comes from a Divine Code generated by an ancient, preeminent Name of God — YHWH. In Gariaev's laboratory, he had already applied LWG to certain viruses, where once their "wave" (hence, frequency) genetics had been determined, he hoped it could lead to the viruses' demise.

Specifically, Gariaev saw DNA as coming from a higher frequency of light energy, what we could call our "light presence" that had concretized into our matter field. So, to him, LWG is the vibrations of the wave field that was once light energy but is now inherent in our DNA information.

At the Academy For Future Science's International European Conference (2012), Gariaev presented a microcosmic view of David Bohm's work on the "Holographic Universe," as the associated waves and fields work from the microscopic to the macroscopic and even to the cosmic levels. For Gariaev, chromosomes are created as part of a holographic continuum, just as a barcode created for an object can be read by a laser. This could also be used for the reading and input of additional wave codes into the human body and other biosystems.

A similar demonstration was seen in the work of Nobel Prize winner, Luc Montagnier, who discovered that DNA can be encoded through radio waves and electromagnetic frequencies into the medium of water. Montagnier and his colleagues (2011) were able to show how DNA worked like data files that could be transferred into the water through electromagnetic frequencies around 7 – 8 Hz.

Adding to this concept, Gariaev developed a process of using and analyzing wave fields for both healing and detection of diseases. He felt he could convert the DNA code through radio wave frequencies, transfer the photon information, and digitize and translate it, in turn, encoding it as a music or an audio book in a type of mp3 or video file. People could then acquire their unique data file to use as a beneficial broadband EM (bEM) torsion-spin Information (TSI). The "collective spin" state of the photon radiation of chromosomal DNA, Gariaev (2013) believed, is a major source for providing image (holographic) information from the gene-text.

So, Gariaev and associates created the first phase of recording biological information into a "library of sound information." When simply listening to the "library" it is generally perceived as noise, as it could be compared to hearing thousands of volumes of audio books being read at the same time. This crucial information, however, is not merely a cacophony, but is based on laws of beauty and harmony. According to Gariaev, these laws are primary and are the principles of our universe that generated living organisms, including humans.

Whether we look at the *chi* energy spoken about throughout millennia of wisdom encoded into Chinese medicine as the acupuncture system, or we examine discoveries made by engineers at HeartMath® Institute who tell us that the heart is the source of intelligence, or others who see not only the brain, but also the human intestines with the heart as a sophisticated nervous system that needs to be in coherence throughout the body, there are numerous bio-musical languages within our body that require a new type of understanding of frequencies and light vibrations to comprehend healing with sound.

The application of transmitting ultrasonic waves through the skin has been used for a long time. Perhaps the first major invention was by our close colleague, Dr. Patrick Flanagan. When he was just a kid of 13 years old, Patrick created his first Neurophone. The Neurophone was designed to induce calming brain wave states. It's a simple device that uses two lightweight transducers on top of your head. The Ultrasound penetrates the mind activating the saccule, the same organ dolphins use to both navigate and communicate. Basically, the Neurophone allows us to hear music without using our ears, but the frequencies he recommended help you sleep and calm the mind. It is also a meditation aid.

The study of the physical effects of sound on biological systems, is now called Psychoacoustics, but it has been known since Pythagoras' time (6th century BC). Now it is being applied to many new emerging technologies that use acoustic medicine and that usually involve ultrasound. One example is the ZetrOZ sam® ultrasound device or sam® Sport which is a device that stimulates the body's natural repair process through the sustained delivery of low intensity acoustic waves. This is a small wearable ultrasound unit that has been found to be very effective for the treatment of various musculoskeletal lesions. It is already known that ultrasound penetrates deeper than any superficial heat pack and, therefore, can affect the body more extensively.

But healing does not end with just ultrasonic waves. Isochronic "pulse" tones are also gaining greater recognition, as in the OPT (optimal pulse technology) along with advanced optical pulse technology (AOPT), including 3 sequences of low energy pulses for skin and body. Results are being seen in terms of the management of chronic pain.

Others have gone much further, such as Dr. Anthony Holland of Novobiotronics, a music professor who "converted" to creating pulsed electromagnetic fields (PEMFs) and frequency-specific oscillating pulsed electric fields (OPEF) to help destroy cancer cells. Holland claims to have achieved a devitalization of up to 60% of cancer cells using specific frequencies.

He and his team have reviewed various frequencies to determine which can destroy cancer cells. He found two things: 1) it requires a sympathetic resonant frequency—that is, if we know the frequency of cancer cells and could induce a resonant vibration in a cancer cell it could be destroyed; and 2) we need two electric input frequencies, one low and one high, and the higher frequency must be 11 times the lower or the 11th harmonic. He believes that cancer is vulnerable between 100,000 Hz and 300,000 Hz.

One of the studies that has been broadly accepted is called Tumor Treating Fields which came out of the Technion—the Israel Institute of Technology—around the year 2000, through the work of Yoram Palti, founder and professor emeritus of physiology and biophysics. He later helped to form the successful company called Novocure. Similar to Dr. Anthony Holland's research, this initial study identified a total of 1524 frequencies ranging from 0.1 Hz to 114 kHz (114,000 Hz) as Palti and his team searched for the right frequencies to stop the duplication of specific cancer cells. Many frequencies were specific for a single tumor type. So, again, it was not a single frequency that was effective but a combination of frequencies. That is, Palti combines several frequencies for a specific cancer type, although there are usually common frequencies in two or more tumor types.

According to Palti, frequencies such as 1873.477 Hz, 2221.323 Hz, 6350.333 Hz, and 10456.383 Hz are common for the majority of patients with a diagnosis of breast cancer, hepatocellular carcinoma, prostate cancer, and pancreatic cancer. Palti's research at Novocure is ongoing but currently has been found to be very successful in using frequencies particularly to stop the cancer's cell division. Specifically, they are able to disrupt mitosis in cancer cells by exerting electric forces on their polar components and are especially effective against such deadly cancers as glioblastoma for which they are approved by the FDA in the USA. We, the authors, feel this is an amazing technology, although we emphasize again, they don't use just one frequency as Rife had sought to find (which highlights a shortfall in his research and the accomplishments), but rather a combination of frequencies that are required to accomplish these goals.

This reminds one of plant research, as according to engineer Jim Dilettoso; you need a resonance to get the sound to activate growth. Birds and some insects are able in some way to provide those resonant frequencies. There is more and more research into the practice of "sound healing," and this book would be too long if we were to list all of them. Besides, we are here to talk about sound and certainly not to give a healing diagnosis or support a specific cure. We ask you to do your own research, with caution of course, because some studies do not consistently work for all individuals. Everyone is different, and some studies are still in early research phases, but some have come a long way.

However, for those who are looking for a particular frequency or two that can heal what ails them, we are sad to say you won't find that here. Every problem is different, and often, some people also require different treatments as well as unique frequencies, such as healing with sound through "bio-feedback" machines that measure the body's resonance system. These machines are now quite sophisticated and oftentimes are not only accurate in their analysis of the problem but also can respond by recommending and often sending back various needed healing frequencies. For others, it may take a "true" healer that understands the problem and often comes up with the right frequencies in the form of tuning forks or "sound beds" in addition to their own healing energies. We don't want to leave out the importance of the teaching of a Voice Analyzer Practitioner who analyzes the voice of a person, determines what sounds are missing in their own verbal frequencies, and then fills in with additional music of sound frequencies that can rebalance their system.

The body is clearly a vibratory antenna, and whether we are talking about the DNA or cancer cells, memory, or body pains, discovering the right frequencies can literally move us from chemistry to sound and into light energy medicine.

To quote the first chapter of John the Apostle, "In the beginning was the Word, the *Logos,* and the Word was with God, and the Word was God." So, if the Word which is creative sound brought forth life, we could expect all life to have sound, or be composed of waves that have particular frequency arrangements. Yet instead of one sound in life, there are millions of different sounds, and perhaps as a word or a combination of many words, each one has certain characteristics and wave packets that make us all unique.

Our long-time associate and sound healer, Colleen Clabby, likes to say, "It sounds perfectly wonderful!"

Then people ask her, "What does?"

She kindly responds, "Anything and anyone that vibrates with true love and healing and music helps that energy."

Colleen continues, "Sound healing involves frequencies, prayers, thoughts, and blessings. Many years ago, while I was praying for my mother who had just been diagnosed with stage 4 cancer, I stood staring at a beautiful summer garden and asked God, asked the love of the universe, how I was to help my mother. Instantly, I received a booming command which spoke to my heart and thoughts and answered me! That perfectly clear, commanding voice told me that 'we humans can heal ourselves with color, sound, and vibration!' For that is what we all are made of, every single cell, in every single Divine human being. It would take another few years for my heart and soul to hear more of that Divine sound, to live my life with my higher intuitive voice and trust that sound of love which comes to all of us when we are at peace with ourselves."

There are many who have used sound healing like Dr. Mary Helen Hensley who had her own Near Death Experience (NDE) but now has the ability to "hear" disease or what is called synesthesia as an added ability to help heal the body. There is experimentation with music on the subtle vibratory network of the human body by inventive resonance. However, understanding the chemistry inside our brains is still important as we know that singing melodies can trigger the release of dopamine (a neurotransmitter that enhances *inter alia*, the feeling of happiness) and oxytocin. Oxytocin is a confidence-building hormone that has an influence on love, interpersonal cooperation, a sense of partnership, and fairness.

We also know that music, and not just unheard frequencies, has a positive effect on heart rhythm and our ability to relieve stress. Heart rate variability (HRV) can also be an indicator of severe depression, which music has shown to improve significantly.

Researcher Vera Brandes has been the director of the research program in music and medicine at the Paracelsus Private Medical University in Salzburg, Austria. She created the world's largest study on the effects of music on depressive diseases and in several other problematic areas. She has worked in cooperation with the Vienna Hanusch Hospital, Mannheim Institute of Public Health, the University of Heidelberg, and the Department of Clinical Psychology at the Ohio State University in the USA.

Brandes, a professional friend of ours, was looking to develop a medication in the form of music that would be dispensed as a prescription: "I am the first musical pharmacologist ... a patient comes in suffering from depression ... the first step is always to see the physician. But then there will be the choice of treatment options: the psychiatrist, Prozac, or music."

Finally, we want to simply mention the work of our colleague, Konstantin Korotkov, who also understands not only the importance of aligning your body to establish a better psychological balance, but when it is out of balance, he directs you to use sound to realign yourself. He prefers classical music to psychologically balance your energy and your aura.

Through practices of deep meditation combined with music, prayer, and linguistic cues producing states of higher consciousness, a harmonic field can be generated that elevates the coherence of cerebral waves into a universal interconnectedness with the Divine Mind. So, as we are told in the Far East and India, chanting ancient sounds can lead not only to stress reduction and healing of the body but also the mind and even to ascension experiences.

Higher musical states can allow the experiencer to leave their body. The great sitar player, Ravi Shankar told me (J.J. Hurtak) that often in the middle of a concert he would project himself into the audience and watch himself, from that place of awareness, as he performed on stage. With practice in using music and sound, a mental door opens for both local and cosmic information through the consciousness field.

Ravi told me: "I was playing the sitar with tremendous spiritual inspiration and had the experience of leaving my body and following the musical patterns of the sitar into the audience where I would sit with my audience and watch my physical body on stage playing the sitar with my fingers making powerful and stirring crescendos. In what I call the musical ether realm, I could also see energy patterns around the bodies in the room."

Ravi Shankar's hope was to augment the experience of listening to the music, to open our minds and hearts to the emergence of new questions that can cross biological boundaries and become new discoveries and experiences ushering in a bio-spiritual music, as a new link between plants, animals, humans, and cosmic realities, that can all be used for the healing power of the body, mind, and soul.

How does this work? We believe certain sounds, especially Sacred Names and Sacred Expressions from the Sanskrit, the Hebrew, the Egyptian, and the Greek, to name a few, help us to synchronize the functioning of the cerebral hemispheres and unleash a highly coherent brain state that optimizes flashes of mental pictures that open the mind to become as a "portal to ascension," as well as increases its ability to gather information in the brain through what we call "pictographic communication."

The Sacred Names reveal that the Divine represents the Universal Mind so we can proceed with the understanding that the Divine Names possess a two-fold nature that activates both Divine Energy and Divine Thought. This suggests that using the Names can give us not only insights into ourselves, but also into the greater Divine Mind. Thus, our consciousness mind is able to reach out and experience certain aspects of the Divine because the foundational structures of creation involved in linguistic formulations are able to enter and leave our finite boundaries.

In other words, the sacred sounds and vibrations presented later in the book can provide access to a higher conversation and higher information. As we enter these new dimensions of experience, the use of Sacred Language helps us not only achieve energetic openings for our soul and physical-vibratory body, but it also actually activates the "super-mind" or "Quantum Mind" that allows us to attain our Light Body. The Names teach us how to reach out into the universal Divine Force of life to consciously break out of these boundaries we are living in. When you come into contact with the highest level of Divine Vibration, you can, through self-realization, find the Divine spark within. Life elevated by a reconnection with the Divine Source (or living hierarchy of beings) can become a synergistic symphony with higher harmonics of being.

So, whether you are in the process of getting healed or in the process of deep meditation, working with various Hertzian waves, you can interconnect the human mind with holographic cosmic consciousness. Multiple harmonic states allow human brain waves to be highly synchronized and elevated to higher levels, in unique harmonic waves, as if all frequencies of all neurons from all cerebral centers begin to play a sound symphony.

THE SACRED CHAMBERS
OF SOUND

*A*coustics or the science of sound deals not just with its production and transmission, but also "sound effects." In considering the relationship of the vibrations of each sound with its fundamental sound, in the right environment, there can also be created a unison of sounds. This coincides exactly with the numerical values already discovered by the Pythagoreans who worked out a mathematical expression for musical intervals.

Let's start with a fundamental sound like OM which is considered by those of the East as the primal "sound" in the universe. The sacred OM utterance has long been used as a sound to trigger altered and higher states of consciousness. This is enhanced when the fundamental "seed syllable" is elongated over and over again in minutes and hours of audible or "inner" inaudible meditation. Eben Alexander heard something similar during his Near Death Experience. While on the other side, he heard something like the OM but of a frequency he had never heard before and has not been able to duplicate since. He realized that the sound put him into a state of higher consciousness and transformed him.

The OM itself can be called a "seed syllable" as it is part of the foundation of Sacred Expressions showing a much larger table of linguistic and liturgical exchanges that, along with priestly music, were to be used in sacred chambers from Persia to Egypt where sounds could be enhanced, especially using the names of certain deities. Sanskrit is considered by some to be the musical "language of the gods" and part of the cosmic vibration of the universe taking on form. The sages say that when you speak or chant Names and Expressions in the ancient languages, you are making a direct connection to the higher realms. But, of course, this is not only to be said of Sanskrit, as there are many other sacred languages that use the same sounds or "seed syllables" that all people from East to West can use to tap into a greater reality of what lies beyond. What we have found in our research is that many ancient musical structures were built to create a distinctive resonance. So, what takes place inside the sacred chambers is in accord not only with a singer or cantor, but also the ability to entrain consciousness into an altered and even higher state by the use of these sacred seed syllables and mantric patterns, like OM or even Sacred Names.

In some cultures, the *Aum,* called the 4-syllable Veda, is used for the OM, as the "A" represents the throat chakra but for the most part it has the same meaning as the OM. The AM or AMUN, in particular, also has a vibration that spanned to ancient Egypt. Many of the names of the gods were prefaced by Amun or Amon. This and other sacred sounds were very important in ancient Egypt. The Egyptian *Book of the Dead*, although later placed on the walls of tombs, was originally sung over the deceased for his/her passage into the afterlife.

Throughout Egypt, one can find scenes on the temple walls and tombs showing musicians playing instruments, and some honored women were given the title "Chantress" like the "Chantress of Amun." Other than the names, the Egyptians did not write in musical notes as the Greeks did, but certainly the frequencies chosen were connected with a special harmonic vibration that worked with sacred geometry which corresponded to their sacred temples.

In the ancient Near East, most languages have no written vowels (a, e, i, o, u), so the language can change based on dialect—for example, an "a" in place of "ê" or "ô" and the public salutation "*Shalem,*" the greeting for peace in modern Arabic, or "*Shalom*" (in Hebrew). The Hebrew preserves the ancient musical sound of the OM that may be due to language influences from Indian-Iranian contact, or possible understanding of the Proto-Language before the so-called Tower of Babel.

We consider there are currently 5 major ancient sacred languages: Chinese, Tibetan, Sanskrit, Egyptian, and Hebrew as spoken of in my (J.J.) , book, *The Book of Knowledge: The Keys of Enoch®*. Hebrew and the other local languages are based on the "root" of the name or word. For example, *Abiya* (means my father is Yah), *Abiyahu* (means my father is Yah himself), *Adaya* (means he has clothed himself with Yah), *Adoniya* (means my lord is Yah), *Adoniyahu* (means my lord is Yah himself), etc.

Music and vibrations using Sacred Names and Sacred Expressions are based on sacred seed syllables or root words that allow us to experience the Divine resonance which has been engineered in the "Human" Temple to resonate in the ancient Temples of the world. Using the Hebrew-Aramaic, Mayan, or Sanskrit in Temples areas, these same frequencies operate as phonetic-patterns or "phonograms" when the acoustic resonances are sufficiently built up and maintained by singers. These areas were also enhanced by special instruments: sacred flutes, singing bowls, tuning forks, horns, and drums.

Certain linguistic expressions that create vibratory or acoustical environments were instrumental in that which was to be said or sung in temples, churches, tombs, or ancient megalithic sites as a prerequisite for higher states of consciousness. Beyond the profound interest of finding the chrysanthemum flower and other Sanskrit designs in the ancient floors and walls in various parts of ancient Jerusalem, we can presume the sacredness was within the structures themselves. These structures were sacred for many reasons, amongst which were: 1) the location on the earth, usually in sacred grid points (node points) on the Earth; 2) the mathematics of the chamber or building created a sacred geometry often connected with PI or PHI; and 3) the materials used for construction such as limestone or granite. These three together established a higher sound-resonance.

So, in addition to wave frequencies, there are unique mathematical arrangements specially related to the sacred geometries. One is called the Golden Section or golden mean, known to the ancients as the golden proportion (ratio) associated with the golden rectangle, and designated by the Greek letter *Phi* Φ. In nature, it has been found to be related to the spiral growth in seashells and other organisms. The ratio is obtained mathematically as the limit of a series of numerical divisions called the Fibonacci series (1,1,2,3,5,8,13 ...), or in India the Hemachandra numbers. The Fibonacci series is also found in the musical scale: on the piano, 13 notes make a complete octave, with 8 white keys and 5 black keys. Also, the vibrations per second of different musical intervals are in Fibonacci ratios.

Some ancient temples allow Fibonacci sequences to be heard, where the root, 3rd and 5th tone have specific resonance patterns. We can see how waves of music and sound emanate out in specific patterns, and there are many patterns. The science of acoustics shows that a natural sound is never isolated but is always accompanied by overtones called upper partials, harmonics of the prime tone, or fundamental. This principle is known in physics as natural resonance and in music as the harmonic series. And most people would agree that certain sounds are more pleasant together than others.

In modern day buildings, it is no longer of interest to have acoustic vibrations, even in churches where we can use microphones and special reverb plug-ins. Yet, in ancient sacred structures, the architects or structural engineers intended for the sound acoustics to be very specific and special for all the people who participated. Alan Howarth, who was doing the electronic sound tests with us at the sites, says:

"In my field research with AFFS, we measured the acoustic properties of standing wave frequencies in both the Mayan and Egyptian ancient structures. The acoustical frequencies we derived from the measurements of enclosed ruins areas revealed the irrational ratios of PHI 1.618..., often called the Golden Mean and PI, 3.14159... the spherical geometry in energy. We went to Mayan ruins in the Yucatan and measured over 200 rooms with acoustic testing and found that over 150 of them were tuned to A = 216, 1 octave below A = 432.

Why would Mayans do this? Well, it creates a harmonious response, entraining a listener while in the room, but we can take it as physics and sacred geometry. How could the ancient architects know this? Well, likely the "gods" told them, which is fine, or they figured it out for themselves by listening to nature. However the knowledge was acquired, it became part of the priesthood of the culture and integrated into the architectural design measurements.

We then went and measured the King's Chamber in the Great Pyramid. In addition to the golden mean frequencies, our measurements revealed PI frequencies. Further research showed the PI frequencies, ranging in 9 quantized intervals from A = 421 to A = 427, and this frequency range, rather than to the physical world, is tuned to the electromagnetic energy waves of mind and spirit. The PI frequencies correlated to the chakras."

This relates to what *The Keys of Enoch*® speak of as an augmented chakra journey along the Nile where the sacred temple sites correspond to the human chakras as detailed also in our musical album entitled *Journey Along the Nile*.

From ancient times, there were several remarkable examples of architectural acoustics based on design. The ancient Mayan and Nahuatl civilizations uniquely built the temple and courtyard in Chichen Itza, Yucatan, so that when a person simply clapped their hands at the bottom of the pyramid temple staircase, a special echo mimicked the sound of the sacred bird, the quetzal. The sound seems first to ascend and then descend. According to Mayan researchers, it has to do with the steps which are taller at the bottom and shorter at the top.

In our sound research in various temple structures with Alan Howarthg, we generated pink noise which is weighted so it has equal energy at all frequencies and provides a "flat response" that we projected into a chamber as the initial test. The best recordings were clearly in rooms where original construction was still intact. Sadly, in the restoration work performed at some of the smaller tombs in Palenque, Mexico, for example, the original vibrations were destroyed simply because they used a substitute masonry which altered the reflective sound patterns. Where reconstruction was accomplished with the original materials, the results were positive. When restoration incorporated modern materials, the resonance was generally lost.

A number of resonant frequencies were discovered to be similar in diverse locations, using both pink noise and sweep tones. Several sites in the Mayan region from Palenque to Chichen Itza demonstrated precisely the same resonance:

> Pink noise frequency showed that three sites resonated at 117 Hz (A#3), four sites resonated at 194 Hz (G4), and seven sites resonated at 216 Hz (A4).

> Sweep tones from 20 to 20,000 Hz showed that nine sites exhibited 259 Hz (C5), three sites exhibited 216 Hz (A4), and one site exhibited 194 Hz (G4).

Sweep tones from 20 to 2,000 Hz exhibited resonance in ten sites at 172 Hz (F4), in two sites at 194 Hz (G4), and in three sites at 216 Hz (A4).

Sweep tones from 20 to 200 Hz exhibited resonance with eleven sites at 86 Hz (F3), three sites at 65 Hz (C3), and four sites at 47 Hz (F#2).

These resonant points "approximate" the notes of F, A#, and C. Musically, the grouping of resonant frequencies approximates an F major triad (F-A-C) and an F# major triad (F#-A#-C#).

Just a few more words on the Mayan temples of Tikal as well. There are many vortex centers of sound we tested, yet Tikal, Guatemala, stands out as revelatory. Tikal, whose ancient name means "city of sound (or voices)," is a living reminder of temples that trigger both the power of the Music of the Spheres and the power "of the soul" beyond what is to be heard with the physical ears. If you stand in the central square and another colleague is at the top of one of the neighboring pyramids, you can talk in a normal voice and hear each other. But more exciting for us is when we were in Tikal in the 1970s and climbed to the top of temple No. 2, one of the pyramids in the main square, leaving a recorder down below. I (J.J.) began to sing ancient Expressions and Sacred Names. As I was singing loudly, a female voice began to sing with me in sympathetic resonance harmonics (not always the same tone, but in harmony). Although the authors were together, Desiree was not singing, and the voice and this melodic harmony are clearly the result of the position of the pyramids in the central square. Powerful lightings also exploded over our heads. Paraphysical sounds and real bursts of light were also repeatedly heard and witnessed.

This is not unique to the West; the Eastern mystics understood the relationship of sound (*nada*) within their temples, too. There is a temple about 150 km south of Madurai, India, a principal city in ancient times. Here one finds the Nellaiappar temple located in Tirunelveli, a shrine to Shiva, who is connected with change (birth and death). This temple was believed to be constructed around the 7th century AD, but maybe even earlier. In it is a unique series of stone musical columns. Although columns are quite common as the central pillars of most temples, in this temple there are 10 basic pillars within a total of 48 columns which are all part of a single piece of rock. Tapping the 10 columns produces the seven important basic Indian musical notes, the *saptha swaras*. The columns are known also as Shruti pillars since they are said to produce a series of hymns and formulas connected with cosmic sounds of truth. Also, each pillar in the temple before the main shrine of Lord Nellaiappar has clustered within it numerous smaller pillars, in all a total of over 161 smaller pillars, and they all make music, with sounds and beats much like a natural stone pipe organ. In addition to the shrine of Shiva, in another building in the same temple complex there are two additional musical pillars dedicated to the Goddess Gandhimathi Ambal.

There are many other temples in Southern India that also have special musical pillars (e.g, Tadapatri, Kuttralam, Madurai Meenakshi, Shenbaga Nallur, Suseendaram, and Thiruvananthapuram).

In China, there is also the famous Temple of Heaven in Beijing, which many tourists visit and are amazed by what their tour guides demonstrate. Most of the sound phenomena is a result of the rectangular stones in the central pathway called the "Triple Echo Stones." It works very simply. If you stand on the first stone and clap, you will hear one echo. On the second stone, you get two echoes, and on the third stone, three echoes. There is also a second echo effect connected with the 193-meter-long Echo Wall, where two people standing at either end of it, very far apart, can whisper to each other and be clearly heard. Uniquely, the Temple of Heaven was built after a vision of "the gods" connected with the seven stars, which some say was Ursa Major, but others identify as the Pleiades.

In short, acoustical physics plays an important part in the inner and outer structures of the sacred temples and tombs created by the Hindu, Chinese, Mayan, Egyptian, Judeo-Christian, and many of the Indigenous cultures—all of which are models for the sound matrix vital for transforming our body, mind, and soul.

As we examined sacred sounds throughout the world, we found that sacred vibrations are found in all ancient cultures. We discovered that the real reason sacred priests throughout the ages have used certain Sacred Prayers and Expressions to help "tune" our being into a higher consciousness is founded in the plethora of derived harmonics. Perhaps the oldest example of sound in the East comes from singing bowls usually made of metals such as copper or bronze that can aid in meditation and are often today used in sound healing. Historically, they were most popular in the Himalayan region and the far Eastern countries of China, Korea, Tibet, Nepal, and Japan. They seem to be a kind of ceremonial upside-down bell and have been dated back to the 8th century AD and perhaps earlier.

With most singing bowls, you only need to touch the edge or rim with a strike from a mallet, or you can roll the mallet around the bowl to get an even more consistent, harmonious sound. In Tibet, they are still used as a meditation aid and to accompany chanting and prayer. Sometimes they would be filled with a liquid, like water, which changes their sound. This has various purposes. First, you can see the vibrations in the water; second, there is the idea of "water charging" where afterwards the water can be considered healing water (but most do not suggest that it is drunk depending on the bowl's construction).

Today, we are able to construct crystal singing bowls which add an additional resonance depending on the quality of the materials used, generally 99.9 percent pure quartz, as it gives a piezoelectric effect, as well as allowing the bowl to vibrate at a precise frequency that is identified as a specific sine wave which is now known through cymatics. Depending on the quality and the size, the singing bowl can even produce a perfect 432 Hz frequency. They are still used, much like the drum and bells in the Americas or the flutes and stringed instruments of South America, the Near East, and Europe.

Getting into the specific research of the sounds discovered by us in the Great Pyramid, it is clear that this pyramidal design was constructed with certain materials that would contribute to an enhancement of the resonant frequencies. In the sarcophagus of the King's Chamber, four points of resonance were produced by a sound procedure which registered at unique intervals of: 90 Hz, 180 Hz, 270 Hz, and 360 Hz. In today's equal temperament tuning, these pitches are closest to: 87.3 Hz = F#, 174.6 Hz = F#, 261.6 Hz = C#, and 369.8 Hz = F#. This relationship was validated by an elaborate series of music testing conducted by engineers associated with AFFS during expeditions in 1993, 1997, and later in 2006 with Alan Howarth.

These, then, are the specific harmonics that were part of an agreed upon tuning intended for the increase of creative consciousness and for the active entrainment of "the human psyche" through altered states of consciousness, that would take the initiate's psyche through increasing states of liberation, creativity, or inner psychological moments of transcendental ascension associated with the imperishable architects who lived in the stars such as Sah, connected with the "gods."

The architecture of the chambers of the Great Pyramid is keyed into various harmonic relationships with the human biorhythms. Although in the past, the knowledge of music existed on a profound level in Egypt, no one understood the full complexity of this until recent advancements in acoustical testing. In putting musical graphs of the first major acoustical measurements ever made together with sophisticated computer software and instruments at Giza with our colleague Alan Howarth, we observed that there is definitely an acoustical architecture in the Great Pyramid of Giza that mitigates the effects of multipath distortion of wave reflection, and that this phenomenon is unique.

Moreover, whether we use sacred vocal sounds or contemporary music cues from electronic instrumentation to test the sound inside the Great Pyramid structure, the music/sound resonance seems to be connected with an initiation process of actual vibrating patterns that are raised or lowered to connect with five resonance chambers above the King's Chamber, which, in turn, serve to amplify sound and entrain the body vehicle into altered states of consciousness.

Repeated music tests in the King's Chamber outlined a root tuning between F and F# in today's equal temperament tuning system. Moreover, the vibrating space is capable of producing sounds in the audible and inaudible regions that repeated themselves again and again in wave patterns long after the tone-generating equipment was turned off, according to Tom Danley, one of the sound specialists who did additional testing for explorer Boris Said and our earlier team. Acoustically, what we expected in the interplay of music with the sarcophagus was found in the successful use of reverberant levels. Thus, the resonance patterns produced in the King's Chamber and especially the sarcophagus enclosure remarkably affect the total body state.

The mathematical-musical relationships engineered in the room or chamber correspond to a steady mode of vibration of the space, which is multiplied in the sense that, at any particular point, the vibrations of sound induction repeat themselves over and over, in time with the body at near points of the same part of the wave pattern. Sound testing from various individuals in the King's Chamber produced several resonances in the room and in the sarcophagus, which coincided at the same frequencies. Resonant frequency is dependent on size of enclosure (the lowest frequency is by absolute dimension). Harmonics, however, are a product of the mathematical divisions in the dimensions of the room.

How is acoustical resonance in chambers created? In the Great Pyramid, the materials of the pyramid are mainly limestone, and in the King's Chamber, it is red granite. Then there are the star shafts (or air shafts) and other openings, all of which are adapted to materially alter tones produced by the vocal cords.

The walls of the Pyramid's sound chamber are massive enough to give the formation of vibrations sufficient power to entrain the human vocal cords or electronic sound equipment into the resonant oscillations. In the sarcophagus, especially, the stone lips of the open sarcophagus and the material walls build up the vibrations continuously so as to entrain the sound produced by the mouth and the whole body.

The vowel qualities of tone interactions allow the Great Pyramid with its unique shafts to work as a large Helmholtz resonance system. Here, the acoustics move like wind across the lip of a narrow-necked bottle according to the air (or star) shafts. Frequencies produced throughout the Great Pyramid have an elongated sound, with notes behaving in differing ways.

We have recorded, several years ago, some of the sounds in the Great Pyramid and other sacred chambers, and the musical pieces can be found on our music album entitled *The Opening of the Great Pyramid* with musical maestro, Paul Thomas Burns. In the music, one can hear several higher order resonances coincide with the fundamental in the chamber—that is, they overlap so that energy can be transferred from one to another. Nevertheless, a precise language is present in music cues that describes the power of the human voice within the design and spiritual nature of the Great Pyramid that positively responds to the prophetic Name of God when intoned by a male cantor.

The harmonics are actual vibrating patterns or multiples, and the sound starts at well below audibility, and we believe the focus is not so much on the overtones of the King's Chamber, but on the "undertones" that are resonating in the chamber. Experiments with mental pictures (cybernetics) while using breathing practices, chanting, and singing with sustained vibrations of the Divine Names can maximize bio-sound coupling within the geometries of sacred architecture, such as the sarcophagus in the King's Chamber, showing the proportions of the human body operating with precise patterns of sound reflection off the walls of the sarcophagus. These sound beats approximate the number of beats of the human heart per minute for an average human lying within the open sarcophagus.

Thus, in a brilliant way, the body-mind-spirit of the "Initiate" is entrained by an overriding ocean of singing, sound, and acoustic resonance, allowing the powers of the psyche to be opened beyond the old behavior patterns. Subaudible levels, when combined with meditation for greater control of the brain waves, create a definite process that could lead to a biofeedback that corresponds with each note and helps to enhance consciousness thought and relaxation.

In our experience with music in the Grand Gallery, we also witnessed the appearance of a strong paraphysical light in the third dimension. We also have seen and recorded several orbs while we were doing the sound research in the King's Chamber. Yes, when we had a small team singing in the King's Chamber and Grand Gallery, standing columnar waves in golden light appeared, a powerful Light phenomenon of which Desiree took a picture.

We attribute the experiences mentioned previously in the King's Chamber to both sound and the inner energy of the Chamber because even without talking there is a harmonic vibration present in the room made by the masonry, the structure, and the openings for Initiation.

We will discuss this further in Part 2 but overall, we believe that the King's Chamber is truly a Chamber of Initiation. Initiation means opening the mind to the other paraphysical dimensions. Using Sacred Sounds with focused toning and chanting is clearly a way to activate these energies especially inside granite rooms which have a distinctive resonance. These build up powerful energy fields as the sounds are elongated and create a continuing echoing pattern of tones, overtones or undertones which put your mind also into an alpha state.

Yet, regardless of where you are in the world, even in your own home, the Sacred Names and Expressions of the Godhead with Sacred Music can be put to numerous arrangements to create greater states of initiation. Although they work anywhere in the world, there is no doubt that the sound structure of the Great Pyramid and many other ancient temples increases their effectiveness.

Clearly, the Egyptians regarded music and mathematics as basic to the structure of the universe, finding parallels between the inherent patterns of music and all types of form. The basis of integrating the whole system of Egyptology—and the cipher of Thoth (the Scribe, Enoch)—is to bring hidden music, the music hidden in our body, to the world. The ancients understood and structured into the vast designs of temple complexes, musical structures both audible and inaudible, structures that were not arbitrary but were scored into the very nature and flexibility of the organic side of life, operating within the paths of the building blocks of creation.

Thus, in the hermetic sense of the ancient teaching of musical theory, you can leave behind the spatial human form and enter a body of Light multiples; you can enter a larger eka universe, which is one plane higher than the *koine* or common universe, which is made up of various color patterns, various membrane patterns, and various biological patterns, which will all eventually be reprocessed and regenerated. It is clear that the Music of the Spheres is scored in the Great Pyramid and other ancient temples of the world to such a degree that uncovering their harmonics and rhythms opens one to a natural praise of the Divine in recognizing the brilliant interplay between music, acoustics, and the highest levels of scientific measurements connecting all sciences and, ultimately, all pyramids throughout the world, as a vast resonance network that can activate the grid points as a portal to ascension.

PART TWO

Profound Experiences with Chanting, Toning, Music, and Healing Frequencies

I was born with music inside me. Music was one of my parts. Like my ribs, my kidneys, my liver, my heart. Like my blood. It was a force already within me when I arrived on the scene. It was a necessity for me—like food or water.

—RAY CHARLES

SACRED LANGUAGE IN CONCERT

Over the decades, we have been involved with leading singers and composers who have lived the experiences of the soul and shared them through the spiritual harmonies and rhythms in their music. Our work with different musical soundscapes has captured experiences of a "greater soul awakening," and "the ascension process" through complete human immersion. Collectively, we have been dedicated to bringing people of diverse cultures from around the world together through sacred sounds and sacred performances, from the Zulus in Africa to the Xavantes in Brazil, so that all are able to feel a Divine spark in their lives.

Through our collaboration with many musicians and singers, we continue to share this passion of musical transformation. In Berlin, we worked with Jocelyn Smith, a famous American singer and composer, in a special celebration honoring the November 1989 fall of the Berlin Wall. With her and the *Deutsches Symphonie-Orchester Berlin*, accompanied by singers vocalizing sacred sounds, we used several of our lyrical compositions derived from the ancient traditions, using Sacred Expressions in various languages of the Middle East to create inspiring music that was performed on November 10, 2010, at the Haus der Kulturen der Welt (World Culture House). Rich, colorful and moving words were sung, not by the most prestigious singers in Germany; rather, Jocelyn had brought together those from the ranks of the city's poor and immigrant circles. The audience was deeply moved by the words echoing forth in the true spirit of the statement: "There is only one person on the Earth, and we are all part of that one body." Jocelyn was later honored for this and other works with all levels of society by the President of Germany, Roman Herzog, with particular mention of her outreach to immigrants and the destitute through songs of love and compassion.

The extremely gifted Alice Coltrane, the "mother of Jazz," and the wife of John Coltrane, was deeply involved with the spiritual tradition of joy and devotion in the sacred texts of India, and we, as both composers and singers, were able to work with her with the encouragement of Carlos Santana, to share our work using Sacred Expressions in a special music performance. We were able to unite our Enochian work (e.g., *The Seventy-Two Living Names of the Most High*) with the combined work of Alice who sang Eastern chants of Sacred Expressions to create a *repertoire* that came to be known as *Sacred Language of Ascension.* This music was the sacred model for a deeper form of "sound and soul experience" around the world where the impact of a cosmic sound experience using sacred language could awaken the unity and harmony of the Living Divine within every person, nation, and ethnic group seeking a musical ascension experience.

Our work with Alice in uniting Sacred Languages of the East and West really came to the fore in a performance at the New Jersey Performing Arts Center (October 2006) that the *New York Times* reported on in an article entitled "Communing with the Astral, Spiritual, and Tuneful" written by a leading music critic Ben Ratliff (October 24, 2006). Our gifted chorus, which included Desiree, sang both Sanskrit and Hebrew-Aramaic words, producing powerful sounds that reflected off the auditorium walls, energetically engaging the concert hall full of people who enjoyed the continuous flow of Sacred Expressions. A mood of great awe prevailed in the room as moments of deep and profound reverence brought together mantric sounds that were both musical and sacred. The toning of the words from our album, *Sacred Language of Ascension*, was to be Alice Coltrane's farewell gift to the world, as she passed shortly thereafter (January 12, 2007). In the press conference that followed the historic concert, we affirmed with Alice that sacred sounds and sacred language used together were a recipe for quickly overcoming violence and ethnic divisions, so needed now to bring forth a "Culture of Peace." Our words flowed as patterns of Divine Inspiration.

So, today, we all stand at the frontiers of new musical sounds of the heart and soul if we wish to use them for spiritual and social "ascension" into "new being" and "new becoming" in a vast world of change that can meet world challenges through sacred sound. Let us be the verb—and reverb—of the Divine sounds of Being and Becoming Messengers of Peace!

Drs. J.J. and Desiree Hurtak

SOUND AND ITS MYSTERIOUS MASS

Sound floats upwards! Yes, that's right: Sound has mass, and it moves upwards. While ordinary mass falls down under the influence of gravity, the mass of sound is "negative," and it moves up. This is a recently established scientific fact, and I experienced it in my own body many years ago.

With negative mass, all music and sound produce antigravity in a very real sense. How special! I have always felt the emotional upliftment and physical alleviation—or should I say, levitation—that sound and musical frequencies would produce in my being, but nowhere did I experience it so profoundly as in the glorious Cathedral of Chartres.

Chartres is a cathedral of sound and of light. Everything in its architecture strives up. Like so many of the sacred temples, it stands upon an intricate network of underground waterways. Dowsers have discovered 14 underground currents converging in the area where the apsis and altar are situated above ground.

Each time I visit the Cathedral of Chartres, I will go and stand for several minutes in that spot where the 14 telluric and aquatic currents cross. The spot is easy to find—my body can sense it; the charge is instant and powerful. The

14 node points of the standing wave will match the vertically stacked node points of my chakra system, and resonance coupling takes place. A sacred communication ensues. I can literally feel the upward rush of energy along my chakras in the spine and above my head.

It was in 1994 that I first had this extraordinary experience in the Cathedral of Our Lady of Chartres. It was my first time in Chartres. I was travelling with Drs. J.J. and Desiree Hurtak and a group of members of The Academy For Future Science in Europe who had the unique opportunity to explore the many details of the church that is said to owe its existence to the secrets of masonry and architecture that the Knights Templar brought back from Jerusalem.

For several days, we would spend hours inside the church, experiencing the acoustic power of its organ in live music recitals, visiting each of its magnificent rose windows, analyzing the statues of characters from the Old and New Testament, such as the lofty statue of Melchizedek at the North Portal, and perambulating through the underground crypt with its mysterious water channels underneath.

The crypt itself has a perplexing feature in its invisible acoustic design. A singer who stands in a few particular spots of the underground tunnels intoning the sacred chants will make the entire crypt resonate with their voice. Each day, we sang the Sacred Expressions and Divine Names in the crypt and the church. It felt like we were building and rebuilding the masonry through our vocals and sounds: the pillars and stones re-enforcing our chants, and the tones and harmonics vibrating and enlivening the massive architecture. Our bodies and voices interacted with an invisible cathedral of song.

The full realization of the power of this acoustic architecture of the Cathedral of Chartres came to me only when I had returned home. Exhausted from the excursion and intense encounter with one of the sacred grid points of planet Earth, I lay on my bed with my eyes closed when I began to hear a tremendous polyphonic sound, like a symphony of innumerable voices, a cascade of musical frequencies that engulfed my entire being. I immediately knew that these are the cells of my body singing! Every particle of my body was lifted in a rush of song that, for a moment of time, gave me the experience of a sacred anointing through sound.

Often, I wonder if those in the ancient stories who moved heavy stones, apparently by sound alone, like the Tibetan monks and Joshua and the Israelites at Jericho, were harnessing the antigravitational properties of sound. However, I do know, that to this day, if I go deep within, and cross what I now sometimes call that "threshold of negative mass," I can recall the glorious music of my life, experiencing true upliftment through sound frequencies.

Ulrike Granögger

SACRED SAND

The sound of fifty monks chanting has opened my heart. I weep as they masterfully pour colored sand from their fists, creating a work of art as impermanent as the echo of their voices.

In three weeks, our tour group had participated, mostly as observers and silent guests, in twenty-two sacred ceremonies in Tibetan temples, monasteries, and nunneries. Sound was an element everywhere we went with voices chanting, singing, calling, bells, bowls, and gongs. Huge drums and minute, hand-held ones. The sounds of wind and cushions being shifted on floors and wooden seats, softening the hard surfaces so we could remain mindful for long periods of time. Quiet sounds of appreciation for warm foods delivered to cold halls. Laughter and friendly bantering. Tibet is a country of intriguing sounds.

After twenty minutes of listening to the monks and watching them create a massive sand painting—silently, magnificently crafting something viscerally familiar to me—I have relaxed into a place so deep and so sacred within me that I am nearly brought to my knees.

I am no longer aware of my traveling companions. I feel alone with the monks and a few Tibetan officials who surreptitiously monitor our group of foreigners. Yet I know my group is close by, sitting with eyes closed, enveloped by the sound and energies of dozens of chanting monks. The local officials have little to do but watch as a miracle takes place.

Oh, my—the colors! The dexterity of hands and wrists moving smoothly and deftly over a surface as it disappears beneath intricate patterns. They create images and scenes depicting sacred texts and knowledge—with grains of sand. What extraordinary artistry!

I feel I am dancing in a realm where my body is not present. I am breathing along with the monks in a cadence of "scoop sand, close fist, funnel fingers, release sand." Their fingers flourish at the finish to ensure that only what is intended lands in the painting. They repeat their moves with each inhalation and exhalation in a glorious, endless rhythm.

The chanting stops before the painting is finished and my group starts to rise, gathering personal belongings, preparing to leave. I am distraught. Nobody else, including our tour guide, seems aware of the magical experience I am having. They could happily leave, not knowing what they haven't been experiencing. But alas, I cannot leave.

I know that part of the magic of this sacred dance of hands, hearts, and artistry will transform in just a few minutes more, when one of the monks will sweep away the truly amazing art that they have created together over the past many hours and days. The lesson is impermanence.

My group is now leaving. I don't like to inconvenience others, when avoidable. My inner, social self is loudly urging me to "Leave now!" But I remain frozen, leaning against an ancient pillar—a solid, wide post adorned with rich, red colors found in many Tibetan temples. My heart is so open, I am barely able to withstand the full-to-overflowing sacredness I feel so profoundly. I am on my spiritual knees, rapidly on my way to lying prostrate on the floor, never to rise again as who I was before this moment overwhelmed me.

I am aware of some of my past and parallel lives. They have made themselves known to me, usually when I least expected it. I remember, with bittersweetness, the lives I have lived with joy, purpose, and a sense of complete happiness. Today has raised the bar on that for me. I feel such an intense longing to again stay with others fully dedicated to peace on Earth, who hold that intention every moment and with every breath they take.

At last, I am able to metaphorically "pick myself up off the ground" and join my companions. I know that my life has changed.

The voices of those chanting monks opened an altered reality for me in the monastery that day, as I observed the sacred sand painting. Both the sound and silence engaged my senses, expanding my ability to witness miracles.

Diane Wilcoxson

CONNECTING WITH THE MUSE OF HEALING MUSIC

*L*ooking back, it was clear that there was a plan for my life, long before I became consciously aware of it. Music became a portal to higher consciousness for me when I was introduced to the art of jazz improvisation in junior high school. Over the next decade, I spent many hours learning the theory and practice of scales, chords, and melodic possibilities.

It was a very left-brain approach. I was consciously choosing what phrases to play over which chord patterns. My main instrument was the trumpet and I got really good at it.

Although I questioned, *Was that all there was to music—an exercise in emotional catharsis, virtuosity, and ego gratification? Could it be more?*

Reading about Edgar Cayce's descriptions of healing music in ancient Egypt awakened past-life memories in me. I wondered, *Why wasn't anyone working with healing music in the present day?* The seed was planted to study all that I could about healing music, and its manifestations in cultures around the world.

At the University of Buffalo, from 1965 to 1969, I studied with musicians and poets who described their own creative process in the context of musicians, poets, and artists in ancient Egypt and Greece. Their secret was making contact with and being inspired by their Muse.

Would it be possible for me to achieve that connection?

As a high-energy jazz/rock trumpet player, I had begun to tap into spontaneous improvisation, "going on automatic" while jamming with incredible musicians. These rare experiences only amplified my desire to make my own connection and attunement with my own muse. I set my intention to do so.

I practiced eight hours a day to get my "biological instrument" prepared to receive inspiration. When my eight-piece jazz-rock band from Buffalo traveled to New York City to record our first album of original tunes, I thought we were poised to follow in the footsteps of the bands *Chicago* and *Blood, Sweat and Tears*.

The session was a disaster. The unexpected blessing was I suddenly had a few weeks of unscheduled time before the next semester began. I bought a round-trip ticket to San Francisco that afforded me two weeks to jam with local musicians and make a pilgrimage to the William Blake Illuminated Books exhibit at University of California Santa Cruz.

To get there I had to hitchhike. As luck would have it a van full of folks my age picked me up.

"Forget Blake. Where you really need to go is to this Zen center up in the hills above Santa Cruz. It's out of our way, but we'll take you there," they tell me.

When we reach the destination, they say, "This is it. Good luck. We need to get back to where we were headed."

As they drove off, I realized I was in the middle of nowhere, two miles up a steep rural road. I could be stranded there. I sat down and prayed for guidance. My prayers were quickly answered when a man walked up and asked, "Are you the person who applied for a job at Bridge Mountain Foundation?"

Without skipping a beat, I replied, "No, but if you're offering, I'll take it."

"Come back around sundown to meet the staff and audition. There's a meditation area about a mile down the road."

As I walked down the dirt road, I noticed that my fingertips were buzzing.

Was I picking up on the natural high electro-magnetic energy field of this land?

Suddenly I came to the clearing in the middle of a circle of giant redwoods. Feeling the need to lie down on the redwood bench and close my eyes, I was aware of hearing exquisite, heavenly music in my head. The music sounded different than any music I was familiar with, but I recognized it immediately at a soul level.

For the first time in my life, I heard a voice speak to me from inside my head. *This is the healing music for the modern era that you have been praying to hear. Your job is to share this music with the world.*

The sun was getting low in the sky, and it was time for me to meet the staff, so I followed the signs to Bridge Mountain Foundation. Entering I didn't see the staff, but I did see an old upright piano. As if in a dream, I walked over to the keyboard and my hands reached for the keyboard.

I began playing the music I heard inside my head an hour earlier. And even though I had never formally studied piano, my fingers *knew* what to do.

Someone coughed. Another sneezed. I hadn't heard them walk in while I was in a trance state.

"Who is this guy and how'd you learn to play like that?" they asked.

"This is the guy I told you about, who is applying for a staff position," the guy I met replied.

"Hire him," several staffers said in unison.

My conscious mind began to question what just happened. I had no idea how to begin to act upon the assignment I received in meditation.

If this new music is really to be a blessing to others, how am I going to share it with the world? I'm an artist, not a businessman. I don't know anything about marketing or promotion, and I have no budget to do so in any case, my thoughts raced.

Little did I know the answers would arrive within a few weeks.

Bridge Mountain Foundation was the second leading epicenter of the brand-new human potential movement. Esalen Institute in nearby Big Sur was the pioneer.

Many of the leaders in the field would lead workshops every weekend, and I got to share my music with them. Within the next few weeks, Dr. John Lilly told me that I needed to do biofeedback research yielding objective data if I wanted to be taken seriously by the media, other scientists, and the music industry.

Did my channeled music really evoke higher coherence brain states than Mozart or Liszt?

I had no clue how to begin to locate the equipment or the funding, much less set up rigorous experimental protocols.

Two weeks later, Dr. Stanley Krippner echoed John Lilly's remarks, but with a huge difference. He had just been hired to be the director of the new Human Potential Institute at Sonoma State College. He told me they had the best biofeedback lab in northern California, and that if I were a graduate student, I could use it for free.

The future course of my life was unfolding effortlessly in front of me. The results of the research dramatically confirmed that co-composing with my Muse did indeed create music with a profound healing effect.

During the research we tested 100 subjects. Two young males had the largest and most dramatic aura photos. We took them aside and asked, "Who are you?"

They were local college students but drove to Cal Arts Valencia once a week to study with Dr. J.J. Hurtak. Dr. Hurtak had just experienced higher dimensional contact and I resonated powerfully with his teachings and information and became a charter member of his first Northern California meditation group. It was for this group that I first performed my chakra-balancing sound healing music. It would be another two years before I was able to record the music, press vinyl LP albums, and begin to share my music with the world, as had been predicted.

Drs J.J. and Desiree's latest research continues to inspire me. In fact, we three are co-producing our second album of sacred chants, mantras, and ciphers, in celebration of our 50th anniversary of working together.

Being in a recording studio for the first time was love at first sight. I would soon consider it to be my Temple of Healing Music. As I attuned to my muse in the studio, I improvised on the seven keynotes of the seven chakras. Each take was a first take. There are no mistakes.

It wasn't until I recorded my first album in 1975 that I was able to begin to share the music with the world. I had no idea at that time that *Chakra Suite* would go on to launch an entire new genre of contemporary healing and meditation music. This recording was recognized in 1999 by industry peers as "the most influential New Age healing album of all time."

That mystical meditation under the redwoods was my initiation into my life's work. Because of that experience, I learned to shift automatically into a high-coherence, deep alpha/theta brain state and play music from that place of peace. When I connect to higher vibrational frequencies, those inaudible frequencies are recorded, as well as the notes I play with my fingers. I've composed, channeled, and recorded music that has helped millions to experience levels of relaxation, mindfulness, healing, and inner peace.

When millions of people listen to the same piece of music, the music entrains their brains into a balanced, high-coherence state. Those frequencies radiate out to the planet, creating a morphic field of sonic resonance that can heal us all.

Steven Halpern

THE ALCHEMICAL LANGUAGE OF PLACE

t was near twilight, and my muscles ached. I had spent the day walking across the Irish island of Inishmore, visiting the sacred wells and Druid ruins. Now having finished the modest meal of homemade bread and cheese that my host had provided, I tried to rest in the chilly, damp room. A peat fire glowed continually in the little cottage's hearth, even in August, because the island stayed misty and cool. But the hearth was on the other side of the house, and despite the layers of heavy quilts on my iron bed, it was difficult to rest.

The sensations of the day—the sprites and the haunting, unseen power of the Druids—opened me to the spirit of this ancient and still-pagan land. My body flooded with the energy of spirits my mind could not interpret. I felt enveloped, as if I were underwater.

The knock on the door downstairs surprised me. The walls were thin, so I could hear my host's footsteps and then the cheerful and eager voices of three or four other people, whom he welcomed into his home. They seemed to be visiting neighbors, men and women, arriving for conversation in their native tongue: Gaelic. In Ireland, the local people call their beloved root language simply "Irish." The island of Inishmore is home to one of the few schools in

Ireland that teach Gaelic. People come from all over the mainland to relearn their own native tongue, which was suppressed under colonization.

The lyrical, rhythmic cadence of their voices permeated the atmosphere. I sat up quietly to attend to the feeling washing over me. The presence of multitudes seemed to accompany this small group of loving neighbors, as their voices expanded and illuminated the air. A gold-white light seemed to shine from their voices.

Languages arise from a place and hold the power of that place. Hearing the ancient language of Gaelic flooding into the home overcame me. Language carries culture, history, and ancestral wisdom. As an invocation, the sounds and rhythm of these words called forth the sea, the rolling landscape, and the multitudes who came before. Each syllable co-created an evolving culture with the land and spirit.

And then the group in the living room below began to sing in the old language, and my wonder transformed into an altered, euphoric state of consciousness. They sang song after joyful song. A choir of Earth spirits, the angels and ancestors, the guardians of these people, accompanied them.

I wept as the music enveloped my body. Awakened by the power, I was no longer tired. I was an unseen witness blessed by the sounds of place and ancestry. The ancient language communed with me and taught me a little of its magic.

Dr. Joanne Halverson

THE RINGING STONES
OF SOUTH AFRICA

"You're telling me that all the stones in this circle ring in the key of B♭ major?"

"Yes," my composer friend says. "Of the sixty-one audio samples you gave me, the recurring pitch is D with the frequency of 147Hz."

I know that 147Hz is a healing solfeggio frequency. In fact, its mirror tones—174Hz, 417Hz, and 741Hz—are the frequencies of the tuning forks I use in my sound healing work.

"And yes," he adds, "all of the ringing stones in that circle are in the key of B♭ major."

As I close the video chat, I am astonished by what he's discovered and can't wait to tell my colleague, Michael Tellinger. We recorded those ringing stones in just one circle in South Africa. It can be no coincidence that the stones not only ring, but ring in harmony.

We have known for some time that the stone circles seem to produce a healing effect for people who accompany us on tours. But this is the moment that Michael and I grasp how this healing phenomenon is connected to sound frequencies. The frequencies must influence the electromagnetic fields of these circles.

South Africa is home to thousands of stone circles, most constructed with only one type of rock: dolerite. The flat stones were piled on each other to form circular walls up to three meters in height. The diameter of the outer circles averages around 150 meters. Each circle is complete, with no gaps or entrances, and stone-walled "roads" connect some circles to each other. Within each outer circle is a unique pattern of smaller, inner circles.

Academics who have studied the circles adamantly insist that they were used as cattle corrals. But with no openings in the walls of these structures, how did they get the cows in and out?

One morning, I tell Michael I'm leaving on a vision quest. "I need to learn as much as the spirits are willing to tell me about how these circles work."

In my shamanic tradition, a vision quest involves spending three days and nights alone, fasting and praying. Michael supplies a tent, his jeep, and a jug of water for my excursion up the mountain.

I feel my summons is coming from a powerful channeling spot where I have received messages from the Anunnaki. This grouping of stone circles sits on a hilltop overlooking many other circles nearby.

Spirits guide me to a perfect place to park. I trek up the steep incline, scamper over the fence, and set up my tent on a soft patch of grass at the apex of two joined circles. The circle to my left is 175 meters across with seven smaller circles in a hexagonal, beehive configuration inside it. The circle to my right is smaller, about 80 meters across, and also has seven inner circles.

When Michael and I have brought people to these circles, they've felt the energy. Some have heard a ringing in their ears, and some experienced headaches if they stayed inside the circles too long. A drone can't land or take off within the circles. We have no mobile phone reception inside the circle walls.

I'm a little concerned because the electromagnetic field is so strong. *Will it be safe to spend three days here?* But my guides assure me that all will be fine.

I set up my sacred space, perform my cleansing rituals, and ask for permission to be in this space. Then I do some site-whispering. My hope is to meet the spirits who built the place.

As I wander around the site, I start to feel strangely tired. I need a little nap. I crawl into my tent, feeling light-headed. Thirteen hours later, I awaken, realizing that four Anunnaki spirits are hovering outside my tent.

You said you wanted to chat. Well, we are here.

They appear to be male, eight or nine feet tall and dressed in cream-colored tunics with wide sashes around their waists. Their faces are not clear.

The Anunnaki spirits invite me over to a small circle within the large circle on my left. They clarify that water, sunlight, and specific sound frequencies create the power to stabilize scientific procedures here—and could do the same for us.

We are using this lab to stabilize genetic modifications in plants. The tones you hear are frequencies that have a stabilizing effect on organic matter. In fact, you can bring people who are healing from surgery into this circle and activate the ringing stones so the medical procedure will stabilize within a couple of days, they convey to me.

They encourage me to tap the stones of this circle, to experience the sound. I climb up onto the top of the wall that surrounds this circle. I have pretty good balance, so I walk along the ridge, about 1.5 meters off the ground, tapping every stone with my pocketknife. I am blown away. Almost every stone produces an intense, high-pitched, metallic tone.

Completing my circumnavigation, I feel physically altered. My mind is sharp; my body feels energetic and strong. I ask these spirit companions if I can observe this circle in operation.

Of course.

I bound off the top of the wall like a superhero. The instant I land, time shifts. It is a similar bright, sunny day, but I know I am in another time. All the circles are ringing and humming with pulsating metallic tones. I see many Anunnaki technicians dressed in long tunics and wearing full-length aprons and helmets. They are busily flying around, performing tasks.

All of these smaller circles, like the one I was just walking around, are *laboratories,* I realize. Scientific experiments are taking place. Three of the seven circles seem to have large bodies of water suspended above them.

I am surrounded by a cacophony of sound. The stones are ringing with a harmonious blend of sounds that seems to be having an effect on the water. In this circle, three technicians are carefully positioning some sort of plant experiment in the suspended pool of water.

The pulsing tones are uncomfortably loud, so I retreat to the circle's outer edge. My guides continue our conversation as the workers go about their typical day in these plant-modification labs.

One of the guides explains, *The circles are containment cylinders and amplifiers for a large column of energy of a particular sound frequency. The pattern of the large circle replicates the shape of the energy of this place on the planet. Using the sound frequency emanating from this physical spot means that whatever we create in these chambers will be accepted by the planet, because it will be imbued with this location's own energy and sound frequency.*

He tells me that sounds slow metabolic function, allowing them to manipulate with a greater degree of success. He draws my attention to one of the empty lab circles that is humming at a much lower volume. *To activate a circle, we attach a pulsing tone generator. Once initiated, the circle continues to generate this sound frequency. The frequency is sustained, amplified, and harmonized by ringing stones that tune to this frequency.*

I can now hear the harmonics being pulsed and generated from the various "labs" as well as what seems to be the song of the entire circle.

We have a team that tunes the circles. If there is a gap in the toroidal energy field, ringing stones are tuned and placed in the gaps to complete and build the energy at that location.

This has been a lot of information to take in and process, and I need a break. I'm also a little homesick. Sensing this, the spirits direct me to a place I will later call Homesick Hill. This hill, about 300 meters from the conjoined circles, has several stone slabs that are big enough to lie down on. The Anunnaki have told me that this hill is a place for them to rest when they feel homesick.

I strike one of the big, stone slabs with a large rock. The tone is amazing, sonorous, and deep. I feel a calming sensation. The sound is as comforting as the tolling of a large church bell. A reclining Anunnaki spirit casually explains that this frequency calms the heart.

Rest here. It will do the same for you. This was a lengthy galactic journey for us. This mission will keep us here for a long time. Some of us will not be making the return voyage. We use this place and the tones of these larger stones to sooth our thoughts and memories, and to reconnect us with our homes.

I realize they carry the sadness of being far from home and family—just like us.

When I return to the circles, I make my way back to the four Anunnaki guides near my tent and ask them to tell me more about how we can use the sound frequencies of these ringing stones to create a healing chamber. One of the guides who hadn't spoken before gives the instructions:

Gather twelve stones and place them in a circle large enough to lie down inside. Six of the stones need to be ones that ring, because the ringing marries with what is above. The non-ringing stones marry with that which is below. This is how we create the toroidal healing pattern. To activate the circle, strike the six ringing stones in a circular pattern.

This makes sense to me. In the southern hemisphere, the pattern is clockwise if the healing requires a release and anti-clockwise if the healing requires adding energy.

The Anunnaki seem excited to be teaching me.

If you want to magnify the healing effect, create the circle out of crushed quartz about eight inches thick. Lay the twelve stones on that bed of quartz. This healing chamber will slow the body down so that you can make changes to the mitochondria and give new instructions to cells. The stones are programmable. You facilitate each healing by tuning your intention to the sound frequencies.

Activating the healing chamber, they explain, sets up a harmonic resonance between the stones. *The more you use the healing chamber, the more the energy will grow.*

When I use my solfeggio tuning forks within such a circle, their sound frequencies will be absorbed by the body at a rate close to 100 percent. Without the support of these ringing stones, you only achieve an adjustment of between 30 and 40 percent.

I'm so excited to create this chamber with Michael and start to work with the healing frequencies of these ringing stones that I can't wait to return home. Our work will never be the same.

John Paul (Eagle Heart) Fischbach

SINGING WITH THE ANGELS

I had known from the moment I arrived at this grand estate that I was going to be challenged by *something* here. I could see beings peering at me through the impressionistic artwork. They were looking in from other dimensions through portals, created by the artist, embedded deep in the layers of paint.

They saw me see them. They watched as I struggled to pull my heavy suitcase up the uneven stairs, headed for the room where I'd sleep. This tour of mystical sites was supposed to be my vacation! I wanted to savor a traditional English tea and enjoy a homemade scone on fancy bone China—not meet a monster.

I took a deep breath, gave myself a quick pep talk, and opened the door to my room. Not ten seconds later, an enormous presence smashed into the right side of my body, throwing me across the room. I bent my knees to anchor myself and drew my hands up like a trained boxer to protect my third eye. Using my psychic eye, I could see my assailant: a big, burly, and wild spirit seething with anger, protecting his so called territory.

He didn't know that I carry the Shaman gene from Siberia. Nobody had ever taught me how to banish an aggressive spirit; I just remembered. So, I did.

Feeling smug, I marched downstairs to describe my adventure to the rest of my group. They were chattering about how delightful their rooms were. No one seemed proud of my triumph.

One woman even said, "Perhaps compassion and love would have been better suited to the situation." Upon hearing this, I promptly gave *that* lady the side-eye.

Later that night, when it was time to head back to the boxing ring of my bedroom, I started to reconsider the fight. As I lay alone in my room at the castle in Cornwall, England, storm clouds loomed outside my musty room. I sank deeper into the too-soft mattress, but instead of being comforted, I felt consumed. The frigid air seemed intent on taking residence in my bones.

I knew the brutal spirit was gone—but what if he returned? I decided to be proactive and ask the angels to sit with me, something I do often. One of them arrived immediately. The mattress pressed down next to my legs as a large, angelic being settled in. For some reason, I was scared, especially as the room filled up with other angelic beings. I froze and wondered, *What do they want?*

I wouldn't find out for another year.

This time, I was with a different group of healers exploring The Royal House of the Sun in Ollantaytambo, Peru. Before attempting to scale the massive rock staircase that snaked up the mountain, we explored ceremonial ruins at the base of the expansive complex. I felt comfortable there. I felt … like a princess. Back home, I'd been going through an unpleasant divorce and a spiritual transformation that felt like being hit by a bus. This enchanting place, 9,000 feet above sea level, was just what my wounded soul needed—a stark contrast to the dismal castle I'd explored the year before.

The atmosphere here made it easy for me to receive waves of hope, optimism, and peace. They were sacred healing codes that I had left there in another lifetime. These inner delights gave way to a long-forgotten sense of childlike wonder, and I began to feel a bit of mischief coming on.

Our guide was describing a healing chamber, telling us how the ancients would place their heads into the carved-out niches in the stone walls to receive healings. Some of my eager companions already had their heads inside these hollowed-out sections. I climbed up into a little stone room, where I felt a female presence who took residence in the energetic equivalent of my spinal column. We began to sing in an ancient language.

As the song poured out of my mouth, I began to cry. I was so grateful the glorious being who was singing through me was able to live again, here on Earth. I had only planned on surprising the group with a song. Instead, we all received a healing.

Two years after my experience in England, the angels appeared while I was taking a luxurious, rose-scented bath in Tasmania. I didn't mind the intrusion. I was drawing ancient healing symbols along the top of the water when they glided in on streams of unconditional love. They felt like family.

Since I was not afraid, they immediately began to sing through me. As we sang, the bath water vibrated and the room became luminous. I was amazed at how easily they were able to move up and down the scales, using my voice to produce the performance of a professional coloratura soprano. Tears were streaming down my face once again. I felt sanctified, like I was a student at the acclaimed Juilliard School and my professors were the angels.

When my lesson was over, and the angels had gracefully departed, I remembered how nervous I had been when they appeared at the castle. That night, I had received a healing to my throat that felt like a surge of heat rushing in while gurgling sounds and mucous came out. When I awoke the next day, I was changed. This healing had seemed to clear out all the unspoken words lodged inside me.

In the years that followed, I realized I could speak in many different languages with clarity and poise. The tones I was now able to create were more refined, like those I sang that sunny day in Peru.

Matured and wiser since that day at the castle, I am more patient and compassionate now when dealing with beings (human and otherwise). I don't feel as though I need to prove myself anymore, because I am anchored in the truth of who I am.

A teacher of the human variety told me once, "Your job is to shine, Donna." It had taken me years and a journey across the globe to realize that I'm not shining when I'm fighting.

My voice was the weapon the angels preferred me to use, to create profound shifts for myself and others. The lady at the castle had been right after all.

Donna Kuebler

IF GOD WERE A PIANO

Music was my first language to talk to God. I started playing the piano at six years of age, longing to find expression. It seemed natural to speak to God through music; I was born into a Jewish family, and our traditional religious services were sung by the cantor, who expressed the pain, joy, and hopes of generations.

But I was never well. I was born with a hereditary health condition, and even though I studied classical piano and was musically gifted, my physical weakness and pain held me back. Unfortunately, I didn't realize that my health was the obstacle. I simply thought I had no talent. Then, at the age of fifteen, I became acutely ill and had to stop playing the piano altogether.

For a painful year and a half, I was confined to bed or a chair and forbidden to do anything physical. I couldn't even walk or take a shower. And even when my doctors finally gave me permission to start living in my body again, I wasn't allowed to play the piano. The physical activity of playing made me more crippled. It came down to a choice of playing music or being able to lift a spoon to feed myself.

Over the years, I tried a couple of times to go back to playing. I missed my beloved classical music. But the result was always the same; playing made my condition worse.

Once I was cut off from the piano, I felt less connected with the Divine. I don't know that my loss of the piano was the major factor, but I certainly lost that connection. Nevertheless, I refused to be defeated in life. I always had a drive to alleviate needless suffering on the planet, and now that I was permanently disabled, I redirected my interests to social activism. I became dedicated to banning the bomb and stopping the Vietnam War. I stood up for tenants' rights, women's rights, and the revolutions in the less-developed parts of the world. I took up labor organizing and more.

Silenced in music and unable to do much on the physical plane, I reached out to the world through words on the economic and political levels. And so, for the next eighteen years, I was engaged fulltime in the struggle for revolutionary change.

Ultimately, social activism was a frustrating journey, and I was left deeply disillusioned with myself, the movement, and my efforts to help humanity.

At the age of thirty-three, God began to speak to me directly. I was an atheist at the time, but I started to "hear" an inner voice. God spoke to me not through music, but through words. This led to a full-blown, intuitive awakening. I'd never believed that I was psychic or intuitive, and I had no religious or spiritual training or interest. Yet suddenly I was undeniably being guided, moment by moment, in every way. My life completely flipped.

At first, I was shocked and scared—but my awakened intuition began to lead me closer to the Divine. I felt that I could see the world in all its dimensions for the first time.

The result was like an earthquake in my destiny. My inner voice told me to do intuitively-guided counseling, although I had no training. I was to intuitively give talks on topics I knew nothing about, and to author books on spiritual topics I had never studied. The voice asked me to lead workshops with no plan or agenda. It was amazing. I was back, trying again to support a revolution on the planet—but this time, it was what I called the "inner revolution": emerging from the inside out and overcoming the domination of the ego.

This work was exciting and fulfilling, yet something was still missing for me—a connection with music. The piano might as well have been on a distant planet.

Occasionally, I let myself feel the loss of my first language, music. Words seemed so limited, so easily blocked by ego resistance. I could spontaneously channel energy as an adjunct to the words, but my fragile health still limited me. The closest I came to music was chanting in my weak voice.

In my mid-fifties, technology became available that allowed me to compose music via computer, and I was compelled to create some albums. It felt miraculous. I didn't know where the music came from. Just as when I was writing or speaking, I felt like I was taking dictation. Once again, I surrendered to the process and created four CDs that just emerged. I couldn't create music often because physically, it was intensely painful for me. The process was also slow and awkward. I felt deeply frustrated.

At the age of seventy-three, God told my husband and me to buy a large, acoustic grand piano. I was supposed to play again! But how? I had tried to play over the years, but I always had the same experience. After a day or two of practicing classical music, my hands and arms became so inflamed, I couldn't feed myself.

Nevertheless, we bought a beautiful, expensive grand piano with a tone that sang to the heavens. I struggled for two weeks to play it, and then I fell and broke my arm. Ten months earlier, I had fallen and broken the other arm. I felt almost hopeless.

The inner voice guided me to a solution. I was not to play for too long at one time—and I was only to improvise. I would play not what was on the page, but what I was guided to play, for as long as my body would allow.

It worked. I became an intuitively-guided pianist. In essence, I was channeling music, and that changed my life and the world around me. I was astounded that, in my mid-seventies—despite pain, fatigue, and disability—I was able to play the piano again. And I was infinitely better than I had been at the age of fifteen, before I became disabled!

I lost all nervousness about performing in front of others, because my ego was not involved. I just communicated through music, guided by the Divine. And that has continued. Even though I have to restrict the amount of time I play, my hands fly across the keys and music pours out of me or through me. I enter an altered state, expressing my deepest emotions, yet I'm no longer just me. Instead, I feel as elevated as when I'm doing any kind of intuitive work.

After fifty-eight years of not playing the piano, I became so comfortable performing that I started offering weekly concerts of improvised piano music, which I live-streamed from my Facebook page. The music attracted an audience. Strangers have often told me in the comments that my playing dramatically impacts their mood and their state of mind. In 2021, I channeled a fifth CD of intuitively-guided piano music and in 2022, I channeled a sixth.

But the most impressive benefits were strictly personal. My husband James suffers from cognitive impairment, and we have done everything imaginable to help him. Lifestyle, diet, supplements, and exercise have helped him, but in the past months, he once again began to decline. We both watched him slip more and more into confusion, loss of memory, and poor judgment. We were losing him.

Then one evening, a compelling thought came to me. If my music could alter people's moods, maybe it could help James' brain. Why couldn't I be intuitively guided to create music that would impact his mind?

I was afraid to be wrong, afraid to seem foolish or arrogant, but I asked James to sit down with me. To my amazement, I was intuitively guided to create fifteen minutes of music, which I improvised for him on the spot. Fortunately, I had also been guided to record it.

This was different from the music I normally improvise. I felt possessed by the Divine, in a totally altered state. My hands just found their way around the keyboard as if a mad woman were playing. After hearing the music, James jumped up and took an objective test of his cognition, and his score went up for the first time in ten months.

Over the next days and weeks, I improvised more healing music, and we both continue listening daily. And astoundingly, not only is my husband being impacted, but so am I. The music has been transforming my health, my attitudes, and my sense of self. And, while our progress is up and down, the positive impact is accelerating.

I have already recorded about nine hours of healing music, and there is lots more to come. I've shared it with others in need of healing. And the more we listen, the more we change. My husband is making noticeable strides with his cognition, and my health keeps improving.

But beyond all this, there is something much larger afoot. As I channel this music, I feel expanded. As I listen to this music, I feel transformed. When I feel this music throughout my body, I feel more myself and more connected to the Divine.

I can feel the vibrations of the piano when I'm playing and even when I'm just listening. I sometimes feel my brain vibrate, or a buzzing in my root chakra, which is unusual for me because of my chronic fatigue. I am alive! Life is in technicolor again.

Despite my health, my age, global warming, and the state of consciousness of our world, I no longer dread the future. I am walking forward holding God's hand, wondering what adventure awaits me each day. And whatever I am asked to do, I know music will be a part of it.

Beth Green

THE GIFT OF RACHEL

Rachel was still in my sister's womb, but while in a dream state one night, I was given a secret glimpse into something eternal and sacred.

I'd been living overseas for many years, oceans away from my sisters in the States. I was at a friend's house in England, curled up on a strange couch, tossing and turning, struggling to fall asleep. Before dozing off in the early hours of the morning, I suddenly began to witness an extraordinary scene: I was watching an earthen rotunda made of rich, muddy soil with clay alcoves. A beautiful figure sat at the edge of a sacred pool, communing with sound. Fully alive and radiant, her earthy skeleton seemed to be made of the same fertile soil as the cave. She had no flesh yet or eyes, but her bones were rich with life, sprouting buds and shoots.

She grazed the surface of the water with her middle finger gently rocking back and forth intoning with great devotion. The sound connected her indelibly with God, like a sacred covenant, to the source of all things. She had brown, straw-like hair and wore a muddy white dress, but her Divine beauty radiated through her connected heart and into her beatific aura.

Somehow, I knew it was my niece.

I was careful of my own breathing, exhaling slowly so I wouldn't disrupt this holy scene. I savored every moment, letting the sound permeate my being and memory with its glorious resonance. I could feel the sparkling colors of the sound energy and its ability to communicate eternity, purpose, and warmth. Witnessing her in love with God, communing soulfully in complete oneness, was powerful. It spoke to me of unconditional love, acceptance, and family.

And then, something changed. Someone called to her, giving a command. Without hesitation, rising blissfully—in full, reverent obedience—she left, and the scene changed abruptly.

Now I was looking at large, tropical leaves that blocked my view. Within a split second, she was back! She parted the leaves and approached me, looking radiant in full human form, her bright hazel eyes gazing straight into my soul. This time, she wore a dress so pure and white that it glowed. Her long, thick hair cascaded down her back. She seemed to emerge from the palms like a warrior of Divine love and purpose.

My eyes opened just before she walked right through me and I blinked in the darkness proclaiming, "Rachel is born!"

The sound I'd experienced was still with me and resonated within me all day. Finally, I got word from my family: Rachel had indeed been born. I was honored when my sister asked me to be her godmother.

Twenty-three years have passed, and Rachel and I have maintained our sacred bond. We wind up in one another's dreams. We delve together into mysterious and serendipitous adventures and share spiritual experiences only we understand.

I believe we're from the same spirit tribe. We are here to support one another in this life. Her strong affinity for sound has remained; she continues to be drawn to sound healing and sound energy.

"I say I'm Divinely guided all the time and I know that's how we are," she told me in an excited text. "We're led by Divine guidance and the voice of the universe, which is why I feel so blessed. I thank God every day that this is my journey, and this is how my soul chooses to experience Earth this time around."

I enjoy standing by as her spiritual guardian, holding space for her and watching her grow and experience different life phases. I don't know where her journey will take her, but I believe sound will be a part of it, because it is such a part of her.

Many years after her birth, I had another dream about Rachel. She was singing a song understood by the faeries. I don't know much about faeries, but I know the dream was vivid and true. I dreamed I had taken her to a kind of summer school training where she would learn the ways of the fairies, and I'd watched her confidently cross a little stone wall into their magical kingdom.

The behavior of the Fae was different than I had imagined. They seemed easily annoyed and short-tempered, but they adored Rachel and softened in her presence. In fact, they gathered around her like children wanting to hear a story, and as she sat on a little grassy mound and began singing a song to them, they shrieked with giggles and danced in revelry, singing along with her. They were delighted with her, just as I have always been.

I feel blessed to have heard the song of Rachel's soul, before she was even born.

Allison Kenny

LOVE YOURSELF ENOUGH TO DO THIS

*W*hen I first heard light language in 2010, I had laughed heartily. *What a strange-sounding language!* And yet, I needed to know more. I found the words to be somehow familiar and comforting.

I learned that this language could transcend the conscious mind to penetrate the cells of the body. The sound could clear, restore, and energize. I knew my own body responded with tears, shudders, light-headedness, and joy when I heard it. Many times, I wondered, *Could I learn to speak this language?*

A few years later, at a metaphysical event, my ability to speak light language was activated. To my ears, it sounded like "baby talk." I was encouraged to stay with it and allow my speaking skill to unfold in time.

For a couple of years, I practiced by speaking to trees, who proved to be a helpful and non-judgmental audience. But I was still self-conscious.

And then, two years later, I found myself behind an old church in the Welsh countryside, being called on to speak. Fourteen of us had journeyed to the United Kingdom on a tour to trace the steps of the ancient Celts, Druids, and Essenes. These ancient people had lived at the time of Mary and Jeshua and had carried his original teachings of The Way.

My group of seekers and Gloria, our tour guide, had walked to a cove near the Anglesey River. As we approached the area, I'd heard a high-frequency tone in my right ear. No one else seemed to hear it.

I had learned that these tones were energetic downloads from higher guidance. I said a silent thank you. In retrospect, I think I was being tuned.

We had formed a circle in what looked like the remains of an old building foundation. Gloria asked us to hold the four directions, and people shifted to do so. She led us through a visualization to connect with the Earth and the cosmos and then bring the energy into our hearts. Gloria played a drum to guide us into further relaxation. All was silent for a few moments, and then she channeled.

"I AM Anna," she said. I knew that Anna was Jeshua's grandmother—Mother Mary's mother.

"In ancient times, I lived here with my tribe. I walked these lands. We spread Jeshua's teachings of The Way. Some of you were with me, but you have forgotten. It is time to remember and bring the message into your world today."

David, a member of our group, suggested that we all hold hands to strengthen our connection, and we did so.

"I guided you to speak just now," Anna said to him. "You can hear me, so do not doubt yourself."

David nodded and was visibly moved.

Gloria, still channeling Anna, spoke a while longer, telling us that traveling to this remote region of Wales had triggered many of us to remember pieces of our past lives. "If we were to cross the bridge back to the mainland at this point in our journey, we would be leaving our mission here unfinished."

But what were we supposed to do? We all wondered when Anna fell silent.

"What is it that unites you?" Anna asked.

"We are all seeking the truth," someone said.

I'd had this same thought, but it had been spoken first.

I had been leaning my head and shoulders against the stone foundation wall but suddenly felt the need to stand straight. My feet were connected solidly with the Earth. My heart was getting warm.

"What else?" Anna asked.

I replied, "What unites us is love."

"Yes, and what are we to experience about love?"

"We are here to learn self-love and model it for others," I offered.

"It is more than that," Anna responded.

"We are to BE love," another group member said.

"Yes, that is it," Anna said.

As the conversation continued, I realized I was whispering softly to myself in light language, to help me to integrate Anna's energy and message. But I was becoming distracted by discomfort in my body. My heart pounded and my throat grew tight. I breathed deeply through my nose and let it out through my mouth over and over, trying to calm myself, but some type of internal pressure kept building.

I somehow knew I was being called on to speak the light language.

Oh God! Not in front of all these people!

I continued with the deep breathing, trying to resist this impulse. Tears streamed from my eyes. Then the words that I could speak to provide an opening for the language occurred to me. As the conversation around me wound down and reached silence, I realized that if I was going to speak, it had to be now.

Love yourself enough to do this, I told myself.

When I pushed past the fear that gripped me, my words sounded as if they were coming from somewhere else.

"Two years ago, I was activated to speak the light language," I said aloud. "I have never spoken in front of anyone before. I'm scared right now, but I know I have to do it."

I opened my mouth and surrendered to the sounds that came through me. Their powerful tone was filled with urgency. They seemed to be saying, "Remember, remember."

The transmission lasted several minutes and ended with a tone—the same one I had heard in my right ear as I had come into the cove. After a moment of silence, Anna spoke again.

"This is the language of my tribe," she said. "The language of the Ancient Ones. You all spoke it at one time, but you have forgotten."

The group began to ask questions, but I was only half aware of them. Someone asked me, "Can you translate what you said?"

"There is no direct translation," I heard Anna reply. "This is a language of sound codes meant to open and move energy."

I had resumed my deep breathing to calm myself, but my tears kept falling and my knees were shaking. Then David was in front of me with his arms open. His eyes held such deep love and gratitude that I stepped forward into his embrace. He comforted me in a soothing voice, like a father would comfort a child. He was crying, too.

Another group member offered me a tissue and I heard someone suggest a group hug for me. Then I was surrounded. I don't recall how long the hug lasted, but it felt wonderful.

When the circle around me finally opened, I turned to find another group member, Kim, kneeling in front of me with the palm of her left hand outstretched at the level of my heart. I stepped into her hand. She toned the frequency that I had ended the transmission with, and I joined her.

As the group dispersed, Gloria gave me a warm smile and a big hug.

"I was so glad you said love was what united us. I could sense Anna was waiting for someone to say it!"

She laughed. "I love the light language. I could feel layers and layers clearing from times when you were not allowed to speak. You pulled on archetypal energy and an ancient will today. You completed a mission."

As we walked up a path, away from this sacred site, several people shared with me how they had been affected by the light language transmission. Some said they had been brought to tears or felt a lightness and opening in the area of their hearts. David shared how deeply moved he was by the experience. I could see it in his eyes.

"I felt the energy come in through the top of my head and burst out the back," he said. "Then I had to come to you and offer support, because your whole body was shaking."

I was surprised to hear this. I had been aware of my knees shaking, but not my whole body.

"You weren't shaking uncontrollably," he explained. "You were vibrating—like a tuning fork."

Jean Fitzgerald Canale

ANGELIC HEALING TONES

had just been in Vancouver, BC where I had a brief conversation with a woman I met about her azeztualite necklace. I remember saying out loud, "I've been wanting to get a piece of azeztualite."

A couple of days later, as I was driving to Utah, my partner called to tell me, "We've found your bowl, and it's made with azeztualite!"

She did not know of the wish I had recently expressed, and I had no idea what it would mean to have such a sacred instrument, my first crystal alchemy singing bowl, come into my life.

As soon as I met my bowl, however, it felt like the bowl had chosen me. The beautiful, twelve-inch bowl was made of pure quartz with azeztualite infused into the crystal matrix. Its tone was incredibly beautiful.

I soon discovered that when I played the bowl for groups, the angels would show up and sing their tones, using the physical sounds to help their energy reach us and attune us more deeply.

My partner Daisy and I were excited to try an experiment and invited a group of people to receive a sound bath and channeling together. Daisy played a set of crystal bowls while I went into a trance connection with our spiritual guides. We were both stunned at what the masters added to our understanding that day.

First, an ascended master named Kuthumi spoke of the "Angelic Crystalline Temple of the One Heart." He said the angels would extend the healing activities of this temple to us when we invited them to our sound baths. Part of my awareness was transported into this inner-plane temple during the channeling.

The air there was charged with healing vibrations. At the center of the temple was a gigantic crystal heart chakra, like a portal of love that represented a focal point of unity consciousness. It looked like the face of a beautiful cut diamond with one large, smooth surface, taller than a human being, as well as many surrounding facets. Seeing your reflection in the crystalline heart revealed how we are all reflections of the one. The temple seemed to be a shared heart space between humans and angels, and the crystalline frequency resonated in a way that the singing bowls helped anchor.

Next, we heard from a guide that many know as Max. Max is a high-level galactic teacher whose presence is anchored in the physical by a rare, ancient crystal skull that was found in the Mayan ruins of Guatemala.

Max explained, through me, that we would soon begin to experience what he called "Earth surges"—energy from the planet's electromagnetic field with a special purpose. This energy would help people who share in the resonance of oneness to connect with each other, remotely, through the Earth's frequency. We understood that the Earth was going to play an active and conscious role in the process of awakening human unity.

A couple of nights later, as I was lying in bed, I felt a surge of Earth energy arise within me and expand my heart. As I relaxed into the flow of energy, I could feel a ribbon of current extending from the Earth's core, expanding my presence to connect with thousands of other people in the world. I could feel the other people celebrating a shared feeling of inspiration and love about what was beginning to take place. The Earth was working to unify us, so that the presence of One Heart could become a strong, coherent field throughout the world, supported by Her presence.

Soon after while I was letting a friend play the azeztualite bowl, the Archangel Metatron spoke a word into it: "Metatron." I knew that the bowl had just been christened with its spiritual name. This sealed the bridge between our crystal alchemy bowls and the Angelic Crystalline Temple of the One Heart. We were now connected through the archangels. It felt as though an ancient collaboration between the dimensions was being restored.

From then on, we shared our sacred sounds with small groups and watched the magic unfold. Whenever we would play, the angels would come and sing with us to attune people with the angelic presence. Mother Earth would strengthen the presence of her kundalini energy to amplify our intentions. She would help to link our hearts with others in the world who were holding sacred space, as we were. Combined with our intentions of peace and healing, an extraordinary movement of energy took place each time we gathered.

As I played my bowl Metatron with our other bowls to create the dimensional bridge stretching toward the angels, I could feel the angels toning to create the other part of the bridge with their vibrations. The overtones in the song of the bowls continued to range into frequencies beyond those audible to human ears. Each time I have walked around a room ringing the bowls for people, I have felt the ladder of frequencies lighting up within me. I believe these frequencies are used to step down the healing and unifying intentions of our celestial helpers.

As this process continued to go deeper, a shift took place. We were no longer playing the bowls as instruments. Our human chakras were the instruments, and the bowls were just crystalline conduits of that sacred sound, helping us anchor the presence of light within us. The sounds they made gave the angels and ascended masters an enhanced ability to play and attune the instruments of our bodies, so they could attune the world through us to the emerging frequencies of peace and human unity.

The tones created with the bowls and our voices have become part of a living technology of sacred sound. This same technology had been practiced anciently in places like Egypt and Atlantis. Playing the bowls with such intention allows the angels and masters to play us as a symphony of consciousness, creating new human frequencies of vibrational medicine.

Saryon Michael White

THE HEALING ROOM

settled onto the daybed, adjusted my headphones, and lay back on the pillow. Then I pressed "play" on my portable CD player and began to relax as the rich resonance of the tuning forks reached my ears. I relaxed my toes, then my ankles, and continued up my body moving slowly toward the top of my head.

Usually, by the time my CD recording got to the crystal singing bowls, I would float on their sound up to the clouds.

Sound and vibration had become my passport to the world of healing. More than a decade earlier, as a participating vendor at a senior citizens health fair, I'd discovered tuning fork therapy as a healing modality. I was attending on behalf of the medical school where I conducted clinical trial research but didn't expect to be offered a tuning fork therapy session for myself. I was impressed by the deep level of relaxation and overall feeling of well-being the sound carried with it. I began to regularly listen to tuning forks and then crystal singing bowl tones during meditation. Through these sounds, I discovered a sacredness and deep level of meditation I had never experienced before. The rich resonance of sound waves delivered health and vitality with each session.

I wanted to share this healing. Over time, as I meditated, I began to envision a beautiful country landscape with a path leading to an underground healing room. The room was equipped with an exam table, a desk, and shelves filled with leather-bound books and glass containers. If I could draw patients to the healing room, I knew, I could use sound to work on their etheric bodies. But no one came. No matter how hard I focused my intention, no patients ever arrived for treatment—until this warm, summer day.

The breeze from the open window swept gently across my right cheek and the smell of honeysuckle filled my nose with an indescribable sweetness. I started relaxing my body to the sounds of the tuning forks. After a few minutes, I began to feel an unusual, electrifying vibration. My entire body felt "plugged-in," and in my mind's eye, I could see a brilliant blue light swirling in a clockwise pattern around my body, encompassing my aura and going faster and faster.

When the energy reached my heart chakra, I became completely immersed—spiritually, mentally, and physically—in the brilliant blue light and the tuning forks' deep resonance. Then I *was* the blue light, soaring upward past the stars, going faster and faster, spinning end over end into space until ... I was complete. I felt filled to the outer edges of my being with *noesis*. As the crystal singing bowls played, I verged on the edge of space and time. Then I began to float downward until I came to rest in the familiar countryside on the path to my healing room.

I had traveled this path many times, but on this day there was something different about the energy and color of my surroundings. I was struck by the beauty of the landscape, as though I was seeing it for the first time. The environment had a special vibrancy. My body tingled as the energy flowed through me.

I continued down the well-worn path carved out of the golden grass that grew in abundance all around me. I reveled in the beauty of hundreds of blue cornflowers as they waved their heads back and forth. The grass and flowers seemed to be moving in step with each reverberation of the singing bowls, and I felt the synchronicity of being one with the sound and everything around me. At that moment, there was no me, only sound, vibration, and frequency. I had become pure energy.

I soon came to the ground-level entrance and stone staircase that led down to my healing room. As I stood above the opening, I felt the cool air wash over my body as it wafted up from the underground space. In that moment, I knew today was going to be different.

Today, I would heal someone.

I descended the smooth stone steps, eleven in all, each becoming progressively wider and deeper. The stone walls, smooth and worn by use and age, glistened with a hint of dampness. I reached the bottom step and felt compelled to look back up the stairs at the opening. A young woman peered down at me, her arms around two small boys. I motioned for them to follow me down to the healing room.

My visitors seemed flesh and blood in appearance, but at times they flashed in and out of focus, like the picture on a TV screen with interrupted reception. I intuited that I was seeing their etheric bodies, as they most likely traveled via the astral plane, as I did. The young woman protectively shepherded her sons, who appeared about eight and ten years old. The mother wore a summery dress, but the boys were dressed in football uniforms and carried their helmets; when they turned away from me, I saw that each uniform was emblazoned with the number 11. As they stood next to each other, their numbers read 11:11. I was overwhelmed with a flood of emotions at this special message. I knew I had to get to work.

I helped the younger boy onto the exam table and began the examination. I could see a pronounced indentation on the right side of his head. He had been injured. I knew how to help him.

I opened the top drawer of my desk and retrieved a wooden box containing a clear glass tube with a tapered, opaque glass handle and a deep blue vial. I removed both objects from the box and returned to the table. I ran my left hand under the boy's head, lifted him up, and administered the contents from the blue vial. I slowly returned his head to the table and waited a few seconds until his eyes fluttered closed.

I took the glass tube in my right hand and began working over the boy's body, starting at the top of his head. I worked down the injured side and back up, then repeated down the other side and back up, working in small increments. Once his body had been fully covered and the instrument was back at the crown, the boy opened his eyes and sat up. The young mother helped him from the table and she, along with the oldest son, walked on either side of the boy as they exited the room and climbed the stairs back to the opening.

I watched them as they disappeared up the stairs, out of sight. I wanted to go after them, to hug them and give them my love, but I suddenly felt exceptionally tired. I moved in slow motion to the bottom of the stairs and looked up, but they were gone.

When I opened my eyes, I found myself back in my room, back on the daybed, feeling the warm, summer breeze on my cheek and inhaling the sweet honeysuckle that grew right outside my window. I pulled off my headphones and laughed with such happiness.

The beautiful resonance and frequency of the tuning forks and crystal singing bowls had shifted my energy and transformed me at an atomic level. I had healed someone! What a blessing! I would continue to use sound, vibration, and frequency modalities in the years that followed, successfully healing many others. But I will never forget my first little patient. I am reminded every time I see 11:11.

Pamela Nance

WINTER SOLSTICE MEDITATION

I have never seen anything so bright, so intense. This place, a mansion-in-the-sky, reverberates with a tone with which I am instantly familiar: the sound of OM. The sound of the past, the present, and the future in its completeness. It's the sound of the universal mind. This primordial reverberation connects me to the Divine in vibrational form.

At the beginning of this meditation, I had quietly arrived upon a hilltop overlooking an exposed valley where I watched the daylight turn into a star-studded nocturnal delight. I rested on aroma-filled grass, which sprinkled a bouquet of its rain-tipped tincture toward my embracing inhalations.

Mists of lilac, gardenia, and lavender floated on the glance of a windy breeze, and I felt gratitude seep within my human frame. I focused my intent into wanting to grasp for more. The surrounding airstream carried a message of captivation. By unlocking and launching my open heart and adopting a position of receiving, I allowed the wind song to share an outlined sketch of where it would have me go.

A noticeably ancient sound entered the space of non-thought, coming close and then retreating, traversing from my right ear to my left. A silver cord became visible. As I explored its outreached, stardust-filled span, it beckoned me to come closer. I knew a journey was about to begin.

Lying back on the sweet grass, feeling total harmony, I realized I was being escalated gently into the enormity of the universe. I witnessed the intimate mechanics of the towering cumulus clouds as we passed. Star clusters became companions, with flaunts of binaural beats and isochronic tones. I remained mindful through this symphony with its chorus of All That Is and I Am That I Am.

Within these melodic echoes, I felt no distress, no phobias, and no distractions. I did not thirst to leave this mysterious, yet captivating, encounter. I felt safe, welcomed, loved, understood, and forgiven. My Earth-suit soaked within this sound bath. I felt cocooned by a devoted transport system. As I bathed in inexhaustible, boundless peace, I noticed no edges and no layers—just a unified and translucent emptiness.

Within this tuneful sacredness, I observed a glistening, antediluvian structure far off in the distance. As I marveled at its selenite crystalline composition, I noticed fluttering shadows appearing above my head. Hovering over me was a solid-white, inherently wise, ageless owl. As this ancient creature circled my form, our eyes met. I knew this spirit animal had arrived to assist. I remain unruffled as this majestic guide relinquished its flight, coming to rest beside me. It extended a mighty wing with an offering to come aboard. I graciously accepted.

I pondered our destination, but in my childlike intrigue, the endpoint mattered not. Acceptance aroused my adventurous playfulness. The owl's wing, which had been soft and flexible, now stiffened with the pulsation of flight. Each flapping motion distributed a unique pitch, sharing a sound encyclopedia. I marveled at the possibilities that awaited me.

My trip was short-lived. I had the sensation of being lowered to a place where there was purpose. I had arrived at the same structure I had previously glimpsed in a distanced vista. This was no ordinary estate. It was a glorious castle of sagacity and devotion. I turned to thank the sacred owl, but it had vanished.

Now here I am, listening to the sound of OM. The reverberation saturates my heart. While I pause to benefit from these gifts, a translucent door opens, exposing an immeasurable, golden spinning wheel. I glance around and request permission to enter, but it becomes clear that I have been expected. I am floating. Every creation around me appears supple, drifting on a current of refined flexibility.

My consciousness is drawn to the huge, spinning wheel, a treasure of sensation and wonder. I become engulfed within its eloquent chant. This is the reflection of pure consciousness, from which I was fashioned. I am beholding…the Akashic Records.

A salty-flow streams down both my cheeks as the wheel rotates with ease, projecting a presence of intelligence. I silently request to be shown my earthly purpose and path. I'm rewarded with geometrical shapes and colors in a panoramic landscape, with picturesque weaves of buoyant timelines. I recall setting my intention during meditation to have this exact encounter. And now, here I am, reveling in the organized data. There are no judgments; only wisdom can be distinguished and gathered.

The silhouettes materialize into configurations and present an ancient scroll. I instinctively recognize its holy and blessed significance. As I steady myself to remove the thick, waxy seals that bind its secrets, the wheel becomes motionless and dissolves.

I feel I have been abandoned by the purest love that I have ever experienced. An enduring composition of music tingles in my mind, and I hear a familiar pulsation. The animal kingdom sage that assisted my matchless journey here has returned. It presents an outstretched wing glistening with crisp and transformed star-dust hues, offering an excursion back to my earthly hilltop. I climb aboard and nestle in, noticing again the silver cord. I know my borrowed Earth suit awaits my return.

I am grounded again on the grassy, moist hilltop. Before the wisdom-filled owl takes flight, our eyes meet for the last time. I wonder, *Why didn't I receive an answer to all the inquiries I had made pre-journey, the ones about my path and purpose here on Earth?* The ancient one points to the silver cord before flying away.

I observe my connection to this luminous, incandescent, vibrational tone of safety. It is fastened between my solar plexus and sacral chakras. Hovering above this tether, on some kind of magnetic current, is the ancient scroll—my gift from the Akashic Records wheel.

A glittery puff of twinkling wind severs my cord attachment. The parchment drops to the ground, where it immediately rolls open. The wind becomes a cluster of green, buoyant light that skillfully brands ten illuminated letters on the parchment.

Before I awaken from my meditation, I read the message.

It says: "Only to love…"

Doncy Falvey

SINGING THE CURRENTS OF SOUND

e remove our shoes before we walk into the Temples of Humankind in Damanhur, Italy, marveling at the extraordinary beauty of this underground cave and the way this world and ours mesh seamlessly. We enter a magnificent cathedral with unique acoustics, every inch adorned with art.

Each of us dons one of Megan's sacred robes representing knowledge, understanding, and wisdom. We warm up our voices and giggle as we realize we are naturally whispering, something we do in sacred spaces. We are here together to explore spontaneous story singing. We are already carefully listening to this temple so we can hear its songs.

Quickly, as we begin to tone, the Hall of Metals speaks to and sounds through us in notes and rhythms, tones and clicks, harmonies and edgy, never-before-heard melodies and combinations. We naturally move around as we tone, and even though our eyes are closed, we somehow manage to avoid collisions. It's as if the rarified energy here has given us sonar capabilities.

Whenever we record these songs, we stop precisely at the same time, a notable part of an organic process creating itself. We take a moment to orient back into our bodies and then solemnly walk away from the central pillar. It is then that we see our glistening footprints made of sweat. Energies from the temple have moved through us constructively all day.

Deep inside the Temples of Damanhur, stories of life through the ages are revealed to us in sound. Centuries of civilizations, countless realms and reaches in the cosmos, all held and preserved in the art and alchemical materials surrounding us now. These energies are flowing to and surging through us. They have traveled through time and space to allow us to capture this experience in a modern recording.

We sing together because we are compelled to do so. In these moments, Diane is an oracle. Megan, a wayshower. Zigola is a priestess. Together, we listen, finding each other. Simultaneously, we listen to and feel the stories as they move into our bodies and animate our voices.

As this is a first-time experience for us all, we agree that Diane will read the stories as the Temples and Hall offer them. She begins by giving voice to what she sees, feels, and hears. Together, Megan and Zigola move into that space of sound, following the lead. It is like we are in one-person hang gliders soaring high together above an expansive new landscape.

Megan and Zigola, side-by-side, pay close attention and follow clues from the glider slightly ahead, in front. The sounds are sometimes like listening to a choir of angels. Other times, they are unexpectedly dissonant. We all move with the currents of sound, listening to what is underneath: Move here! Watch that updraft. That was a surprise! Calmly. Ooo, that was a tricky bit!

The sounds we are co-creating start to buck and weave, soothe and challenge. Our voices meet and part, soar and dive, conflict and resolve. Our tones raise so high, it feels as if the hairs on our heads might part from our scalps. Our tones also go so low, it's as if the Earth will tear apart under the temple floor and mud, crystals, water, and gold will start gushing into the hall.

We tone three different mastery expressions, knowing that the corresponding robe each of us wears is lending a unique quality to our tonal narrative. Keying in psychically to the temple and how It wishes to start our joint journey of tones and rhythms, we begin each song when we feel it is time and then our notes, together, find and tell the story. These sounds speak of love, mastery, Divinity, and humanity.

We feel wonder and know, at a deep level, what a privilege it is to explore the songs of life that this Hall is sharing with us. We are grateful and humbled by the experience. For days afterwards, we move about in sacred energies, marveling at extraordinary shifts each of us can sense taking place within ourselves and each other. Our molecules have been agitated and rearranged by this process.

A year later, we return to this spot. This time, we record thirty-three songs of mastery in the Labyrinth Hall of Damanhur. The songs reflect a great many myths and truths of the ages that directly parallel what Megan and Diane do in their own work and together. Zigola lives full-time in the Damanhur community. We are grateful that she joins in again while also lending valuable input to the recording process.

This time, we replicate the process from the previous year. We don the robes in sequence and the Labyrinth Hall selects the many stories it sings through us.

We are singing stories focusing on thirty-three mastery expressions humans can explore. Some of the sounds coming from us, individually and in trio, are like nothing any of us has heard before. We are astounded by our emotional response: Pleased. Surprised. Delighted. Perplexed. Amazed. Curious. Eager to understand. Seeking more of the same.

Here, we sing in one spot without moving. The recording equipment is more extensive and super-sensitive this time. The Labyrinth Hall is much larger and more cavernous than the Hall of Metals. The technological challenges are bigger and new to the recording crew.

After hours of communion with the stories, histories, and wisdom of the Labyrinth Hall—and our willingness to smoothly move with myriad impulses of co-creativity—we climb up from the underground. We are greeted by cool night air and star-filled skies. All of us are full-to-overflowing with expressions of mastery we have just marinated in through sound and time, in concert with this amazing temple.

It is special and sacred that we can do this as three friends who are also peers in sound and transformative work. The music we co-create is magical. It is transformative. The whole process is a unique journey. We each feel deep gratitude to Damanhur and the individuals who helped us manifest this extraordinary experience.

Diane Wilcoxson and Megan Wagner

CRAB NEBULA AND INDIRA'S NET

*M*y early life was filled with trauma. By the time I was twelve, I was having periods of dissociation that terrified me. I didn't know what was happening or anyone I could ask. Each time I mentally "disconnected" from the world, I would repeat over and over that nothing weird was happening and soon I'd be safe again. I hoped my repetition of this mantra would make it come true.

By the second half of high school, the injustices and cruelty I saw in the world, and my continuing trauma at home, made me contemplate suicide. I had no faith. All around me, people attended religious services and then, as soon as they left the building, they seemed to me to be gossiping and plotting against their family, friends, and neighbors.

I wanted to scream, "Didn't you hear anything the priest/rabbi/minister just said?"

I felt powerless to change. I gave myself two years. If I couldn't find a good reason to keep living, I would go through with my plan to end my life.

I kept searching for a religion or philosophy that would help me deal with this prolonged dark night of my soul. And then, through a series of coincidences, I found myself at a Buddhist meeting where a roomful of people chanted *Nam Myo Ho Renge Kyo* as their mantra. The congregation was incredibly diverse... but they all seemed genuinely happy, lit up from the inside with hope and joy.

I made this my personal mantra. It helped me overcome fear when my stepfather went on one of his drunken, verbally abusive rages, and when I was hitchhiking to my friend's house out in the country.

Exactly two years later, in the community college's packed restroom, I spotted a girl I knew from high school who had been at that first Buddhist meeting. Without thinking, I screamed, "Where the heck are those Buddhists? I've been looking for them for two years!"

She calmly invited me to a Buddhism meeting that night.

Arriving at the meeting, I heard almost 100 people chanting in unison. I started weeping uncontrollably. I knew that I had come home. The room was filled with joy and peace, and I had a deep, kinesthetic sense of my connection with every person there. I didn't yet know what the chant meant or any of the principles of Buddhism, but I had never before felt such high-voltage, positive energy from a group of people. I started chanting and studying every day, and a few weeks later, I officially became a member of the community.

Through my fifty years of Buddhist practice, I've come to understand how deeply my life impacts the world and how my interactions ripple out in ways I will never know. I've tried my best to be loving and compassionate with myself and everyone else. I've come to know the power of my determined prayer and how that's amplified a thousandfold among groups of people who are praying to lift one another up.

I know when I'm feeling depleted or anxious, I need to reconnect to Spirit and elevate my life condition. It's like stopping at the electric charging station with my car. No matter how much rage, guilt, or fear I feel, within a few minutes of chanting *Nam Myo Ho Renge Kyo*, my energy zooms up to a higher vibration that completely changes my perspective.

I suddenly feel more empowered to change my situation from the inside out. I can either ruminate about obstacles and unpleasant people I encounter in my daily life, or I can chant and take the "express elevator to Buddhahood."

When I sit down at my altar in the morning and evening, I chant to my Gohonzon, a mandala that embodies the law of *Nam Myo Ho Renge Kyo*. This mandala serves as a mirror to help me perceive the true nature of my life. It helps me discover how to align my human, earthly desires to bring forth my own innate Buddhahood. As I do this, I evoke a strong desire to help others overcome their suffering as well, so that together we can create a better world.

Many times when I chant, the characters on the Gohonzon seem to start vibrating, and become more bold, and I feel as if I've been transported through a portal to a deep sense of connection with the cosmos itself. It feels like the expansiveness of the Hubble Space Telescope picture of the Crab Nebula, which always reminds me of the infinite possibilities of our own Buddhahood, throughout time and space, combined with an image of Indira's Net, the metaphor for the interconnectedness of everything in the universe.

When I'm through this portal, everything feels possible, and I know my chanting can send powerful determinations out to the universe, where they will gather more energy and allies. This is how thoughts transform from possibility (waveform) to physical reality (particle). I am positive there is absolutely no corner of the universe that my sincere chanting does not reach.

Buddhism has transformed my life. Through chanting, I've come to a much greater acceptance of myself as a "work in progress." I openly share with others my experience with self-doubt, feelings of unworthiness, and my anger at injustice. I describe how freeing it is to let go of perfectionism.

Being a "work in progress" is not an excuse for my failings; it's more like a permission slip to be vulnerable, so that my imperfection doesn't keep me from trying my best to make the world a better place.

Chanting *Nam Myo Ho Renge Kyo* is my all-purpose tool to navigate and savor the great mysteries of life.

Deborah Ann Bustin

VIBROACOUSTIC ASTRAL TRAVEL

atching a video of physician and scientist Hans Jenny sending sine wave frequencies through water, I first learned about the power of sound. I was mesmerized as a container filled with water and orange oil swirled and the chaotic blobs became more organized, forming beautiful, geometric patterns.

Soon after I saw that video, a chain of synchronicity led me to discover a niche in the field of sound healing called "vibroacoustics"—*vibro* meaning "to feel," and *acoustics* meaning "to hear." I began working in sales for an international distributor of consciousness technologies and I was required to test the different vibroacoustic devices. I did so gladly, eager to experience a device firsthand.

Reviews of this technology described deep relaxation, altered states, remote viewing, and out-of-body experiences. I was a little nervous, but mostly excited to try!

A coworker assisted me in setting up the session. I lay on my back on a mat placed on the floor. That device was basically the top of a massage table fitted with sound transducers. It was connected to technology that would drive the music and sound waves into the device.

My associate covered me with a light blanket and put headphones over my ears and a small pillow over my eyes to block light. The moment he turned the sound mat on, I felt and heard the slow, soft music, which I knew was embedded with binaural beat frequencies. My legs and torso began to pulsate. It felt like being gently rocked, a soothing sensation.

My breathing slowed, and within a couple of minutes, I stopped analyzing what was happening. I felt like I was wrapped in a cocoon of sound, internally and externally. It was unlike anything I'd ever felt before. I forgot I was at work and lost touch with my physical surroundings. Behind my closed eyes, I started to see a vivid display of colors: red, orange, blue, and purple. Dynamic patterns flickered like the northern lights against a dark night sky.

Suddenly, my consciousness radically shifted. My astral body began to fly. I could see that I was about twenty minutes south of where I worked. From high in the air, I looked down at the Golden Gate Bridge, which spans the San Francisco Bay. Startled and momentarily afraid, I wondered, *Am I still breathing?* But an instant later, it no longer mattered, because I was surrounded by pure, ecstatic, free, and expansive love.

Instead of fear, now I felt empowered. I was certain that something existed beyond my five senses, and I was in contact with it. I was having a Divine experience with the infinite intelligence of the multiverse.

I seemed to be hovering slightly northwest of the bridge. The perspective gave me a bird's-eye view of the whitecap water flowing in the bay. I could not feel the wind, even though I knew it was causing the ripples in the water. Few clouds blocked the bright afternoon sun, but I could not feel the heat. Somehow, I knew an aspect of myself was looking down on the bridge but another part of me was simultaneously watching me do that. I was both experiencing and watching it happen.

Back at the office, my concerned coworker had lifted my still hand and set it down again gently. With a jolt, I returned to my body; I felt shaken, as if

I'd had a bumpy landing. *Where am I now? Oh, that's right, I'm at work, lying on a sound mat on the carpeted floor in the conference room.*

My colleague said he had become a little worried when my breathing changed and my body went limp. He wanted to make sure I was okay. He removed my headphones and eye pillow and turned off the sound mat. I continued to slowly oscillate for a while, even with the device off.

"How long was this session?" I asked.

"About ten minutes," he replied.

I told him in detail about everything that had happened, still feeling the euphoria of my out-of-body "flight." I could see from his expression that he was eager and ready to try this technology himself.

Something important had just transpired. I had confirmed for myself that the use of sound was extraordinary! My experience marked a turning point in my life and became the catalyst for a major transformation. I knew then that I would seek professional training and become a sound healing practitioner.

Debra Laforest

AN EQUINE SOUND BATH

*W*ould a horse benefit from a sound bath? This question became a spirit-led quest for me after a close friend and her husband arranged for a group coaching session with therapy horses.

My friend Kate is an Equine-Partnered life and business coach who works with the assistance of horses and goats. Her fifteen-acre ranch is home to two special mares: Phoenix and Celita. These therapy horses communicate with Kate about their perceptions of her human clients, describing what they think we are processing or what we might be needing to understand about ourselves on a deeper level.

Kate's mares are sentient beings full of grace and wisdom. I was immediately struck by the energy of their extreme presence as they observed our human tribe.

They stood almost motionless, holding the frequency of stillness like Zen masters. I felt humbled to be in their sight when these towering animals slowly approached our circle. They seemed totally relaxed while standing; each had a back, right hoof gently bent forward and their heads were down, nose to nose, as if they were in a huddle whispering to each other.

Quietly, their huge brown eyes rolled over each of us as we sat in a circle in our camping chairs. The horses' energy fields were as mountainous as the snow-capped peaks which hovered above their manes in the distance. At one point, I felt them reading into my energy field as I was reading into theirs. My heart remained open and curious throughout the session.

Although Phoenix is the alpha, I could tell that she was holding onto an old trauma around loud noises from an aggressive past owner. This was never translated or validated, but I knew it intuitively. I had felt it the moment she came into the paddock. She was uncertain and a bit anxious around new sounds.

One year later, I returned to the ranch. I had come equipped with something therapeutic for Phoenix. In the paddock, I placed three crystal bowls on a sturdy table and set up my phone behind me to capture the animals' reactions when I began to play.

It was incredibly windy that day, which can irritate and disorient a horse's senses. Phoenix and Celita would pop their heads in and out of the barn, but they seemed somewhat distracted. I could feel Celita's energy passively focused on Phoenix; it was as if I was observing an energetic coaching message from one horse to another. I was only an observer, playing my bowls while silently listening to their banter.

Kate encouraged Phoenix to come back into the barn and listen to the sound healing, but the horse seemed a bit uncertain about what to do. She stayed to listen for a little while, but I could feel her discomfort.

"It's okay," I whispered to her.

Phoenix walked out and shook off a long wave of energy; it looked like an undulating trail under her brown-and-white spotted fur. I know she's skilled at releasing energy via yawning or other motions, but this was a different type of reaction. The bowl I was playing was in the key of C, which is attuned to the heart chakra frequency. She seemed to be moving the energy of her trauma through her own energy body!

Kate and I both witnessed Phoenix's response as the horse headed outside to integrate and process what she had just experienced. I knew therapy horses were trained to give their energy, but I wondered if they could receive it as well. *Is it possible that we share similar chakra fields with the four-legged?*

I continued playing for an hour, performing a sound healing to replenish the energy fields of a couple of hard-working equine masters. Celita tenderly popped her head in to say hello when I saw that Phoenix had wandered out into the field. The crystal bowls I had brought represented the energies of the third eye, the heart, and the root chakras. Celita bowed her head slightly and closed her eyes, taking in all these unusual new frequencies.

She moved her body slightly, allowing for more of the sound bath to penetrate her field. After fifteen minutes or so, she slowly turned her body to back up toward the bowl on my far right, the bowl whose tone was aligned with the root chakra. I watched in utter amazement. It was as if Celita was absorbing the healing frequencies from the sound bowls and saying, "Fill me up!" Kate commented that Celita likes to help heal her clients by using the energy of her root chakra.

I could feel this gentle mare delivering healing by demonstrating what being more grounded feels like, energetically speaking. Her energy felt receptive and soft. Her mesmerizing, midnight pupils reflected only present-moment awareness. She worked to help humans awaken to themselves.

As I played, I spoke to her aloud about each bowl. She amplified the validity of the healing frequency emitting from the bowls by taking what she needed to replenish her own energy body. When she was satiated, she glided outside to soak up the last bits of a waning sunset.

When I started to pack up my things, Phoenix wandered back into the barn. She put her nose inside one of my bowls and looked up at me. I assured her she didn't have to be afraid of these new sounds. "The bowls have healing frequencies to soothe the rough parts inside of us," I explained.

She nodded her head a few times in agreement.

We chatted back and forth like old friends. Kate laughed with delight that I was having a rapport with her animals.

"I think Phoenix is ready to move through her old anxiety of whatever she is carrying energetically," I told Kate. "That's why she came back into the paddock. She wants to try again."

I told Phoenix I would bring my third chakra bowl next time, to help her through any stuck energies surrounding fear. We are building trust, Phoenix and I. It takes time. Trust must be earned, even with animal souls.

Michelle McClennen

SOUND LIFE REGRESSION

orking in a crystal store in the East Village of New York City, I learned about the metaphysical from the owner, a man I sometimes call my uncle. I knew music kept me in a meditative, analytical state, but I'd never heard of sound healing until he told me his younger brother, Alfonso, performed such healings.

My uncle had an apartment a couple of blocks away that they used for their sessions. When I arrived, the place smelled of sage and palo santo, and I saw a massage table with chakra lights on top of it as well as a gong and singing bowls.

Alfonso told me to lie on the table and relax. The whole room was dim. When he hit the gong, I instantly plunged into complete darkness. I still felt connected to my body, but only by a slender thread. As he played the gong, the sound vibrated through my body. I could feel my cells and organs vibrating as well. This higher vibration was releasing my soul into the astral plane. My ego kept battling it, trying to jump back into my body out of fear, until he started using the singing bowls.

The bowl was close to my ear when he tapped it, and I felt like my soul was a bouncing ball soaring up out of my body. Suddenly, I could see myself in different bodies in different time periods. In one lifetime, I was a child living in a Shaolin temple. I was running toward other Shaolin monks, calling to them.

I also saw a vision of myself in a jungle, but I couldn't determine its location. In my last vision, I was high up in space, just floating among the stars.

The version of me wearing Shaolin clothes reappeared, his aura glowing with an orange/yellow light. "You have lived several lifetimes," he told me. "Now is the time to learn, so you will not have to repeat these lessons. You will enter a new life, a rebirth."

Alfonso placed a sound bowl on my stomach and struck it—and the Shaolin monk transformed into light energy. I heard my own voice calling, "Continue the mission. You know what it will be."

After a few minutes, Alfonso removed the sound bowl and played a few chimes, and then the room went silent.

"Slowly come back to your body," Alfonso said. "Move your fingers and toes."

I dropped back into my body and opened my eyes, feeling a sense of purpose. I knew sound had awakened me to my purpose by relating a message from my past self.

"I saw you visit past lives," Alfonso said. "And a being spoke to you."

"Yes. That being was me."

Elijah Negasi

MY FRIEND THE TREE SPIRIT

I had just joined a soulful group out of Portland, Maine. Led by our teacher, Rachael, we would have workshops where we went on field trips to meet other local people who'd had spiritual experiences or had guidance to share with us.

I hadn't met any of the other group members yet and was a little nervous. At my first meeting, three women, including Rachael, showed up at the home of Deborah, Rachael's friend.

Deborah was a beautiful young woman who worked with sound. She directed all of us to get comfortable sitting in a circle and brought a big crystal into the circle for energy.

"We're going to do a sound meditation where we connect with a tree spirit," she told us.

This was all new to me, I didn't know about tree spirits, or sound meditation, but Deborah seemed pleasant and kind. She had a way of making everyone comfortable.

Deborah introduced us to several tuning forks, explaining the frequencies each one produced. She instructed us to join hands and close our eyes and let the vibrations of each tuning fork flood into our space. The sound itself resonated within our circle; we could feel the vibrations flowing through us.

At the end of the tuning fork meditation, Deborah sang a chant in the Greek language. Music has been an important part of my life, but I had never heard sounds as beautiful as those our host was creating. It was as if the angels were singing to us that day. Her voice enveloped us in a warm, beautiful blanket of sound for about ten minutes, giving us all goosebumps. The vibrations flowing through us felt timeless. We were completely lost in the moment as these angelic sounds resonated within our souls.

Then Deborah asked us to keep our eyes closed and sing sounds that just came to us as we visualized a connection with a tree spirit. She told us she would be going around our circle behind each of us and would touch us on the shoulder as we made our sounds.

I suddenly could hear myself chanting a song in some unknown language. I tried to visualize the wonderful pine grove in the front of my house—but something wasn't working. I wasn't connecting with anything.

Suddenly, I remembered a maple tree I used to climb when I was a child. It grew on my parent's property, in the town where I grew up. Its branches were perfect for climbing.

I lived on a country road, and I loved to visit the maple's upper branches, just to be by myself. It always brought me peace. That tree was a place I could escape, be still, and just be. Most of the time, I would scale it to the top and enjoy the beautiful view. I could even see the city of Boston in the distance!

While I was thinking about the pine grove of where I currently live, somehow, this maple tree found me. I realized that the maple and I have always had a connection; it was just that I had grown up and forgotten. I was communicating with this tree spirit telepathically, through feelings and images.

The tree had its own message for me. It explained that it always enjoyed my presence and was careful to make sure I never fell from its branches.

Tears started flooding my eyes. Even though I was chanting in an unknown language, in the presence of people I had just met, I didn't feel self-conscious.

The maple tree loved me and was happy to see me again. I could feel its joy. I told this tree I loved him, but he knew anyway, because we both felt the same love. We shared a special moment where we felt the love of each other's presence, as if we were one spirit. The beautiful, emotional moment was bittersweet. How I missed that tree! I had a sad feeling that the tree no longer stood in my parents' yard. Yet I could still touch into these childhood memories of a tree I loved to climb, which evidently loved me climbing it.

After the meditation, we each took turns describing our experiences. My teacher, Rachael, said she had noticed that I was crying during the sound meditation, as well as chanting.

"I just started singing spontaneously," I explained. "I have no idea where it came from or what I was saying."

Rachael said I might have been speaking the language of the Sioux tribe of Native Americans.

"I wanted to connect with my pine grove, but instead I was brought back to a childhood memory of a tree I loved to climb," I said, crying again.

"Is that tree still alive?"

"I'm not sure, but I don't think so."

A few weeks later, I visited my parents and noticed the maple tree was no longer there. My mother told me they had cut it down. I was sad that it was gone, but happy that the tree and I seemed to remember each other. That means my friend the tree spirit will never die. His spirit lives in me forever.

Soon after, I had a mystic friend read my Akashic Records and found out I had been Native American in three past lives. That explained my love for nature and why I used to walk in the woods for hours when I was younger, watching the animals, feeling the scents and sounds of nature. In one life, I was a medicine man in the tribe of the Oglala Sioux, and in others, I'd been a female Apache and female Cherokee. The sound meditation, by restoring contact with my tree spirit, had reawakened my sense of peace and harmony with nature.

I can still smell that maple and hear the sound of the wind through its leaves. I can feel the bark and the loving embrace of the branches beneath me. I will never forget the sense of oneness I shared with my friend, the tree spirit.

Jeffrey E. Washer

A MUSICAL EXPERIENCE WITH DEMENTIA PATIENTS

I had finished a training program that taught me how to play my guitar as a tool for healing and "Romp Down Memory Lane" was a one-man show I put together for dementia patients in memory care facilities. These patients benefit from "familiar" songs and melodies, so I incorporated sing-along songs, early pop music from the days of the transistor radio, upbeat early pop tunes, and country music. I was privileged to see firsthand how these songs—plus a few hymns and patriotic songs—got the attention of patients who responded to almost nothing else.

I played the songs in my show in nearly the same order each time I visited. In one facility, I played these songs in an intimate, living room setting once every two weeks for a couple of years.

Some of the residents in my audience had diminished speech capabilities, as well as memory loss. They were clinically "demented." Yet I witnessed firsthand that dementia includes a great range of states of being and mental/ physical capabilities.

My dorky little "show" consisted of lots of jokes (on me) and just trying to have fun. I studied the era of Red Skelton, Dick Van Dyke, and Lucille Ball to learn this kind of humor to connect with the audience.

In playing songs from the "American Songbook" and some top-forty songs, I discovered that the human body seems to respond best to music in 3/4 time. My audience members would sway to this waltz beat when I played a well-known melody. The music seemed to reach inside their minds. I always started with a "sing-around-the-campfire" type song in 3/4 time—for example, "Home on the Range"—and moved on from there.

Even the folks who were normally head-down and drooling, sitting in wheelchairs, would sometimes tap their fingers in rhythm. They might eventually bring their heads up or even make eye contact, and occasionally, I got a smile. Not from all of them, and not all the time—but when it happened, it was a remarkable and precious experience.

My performing talent is not stellar by any means. I don't believe the healing benefit of these shows was a product of my musical skill or singing ability. It was more the fact that I showed up and gave every performance my best intention and effort. I stayed aware of my audience and their needs. This was not about me.

I sang patriotic songs, even when I was furious at our government. I played religious songs for them while not participating in organized religion. These gigs were not an avenue for me to express my artistic self, or even my musical skill, beyond the most basic ability to strum some chords and hold a melody. I had to keep it simple to even pull it off.

Sometimes, it worked. One fan of the shows was a veteran named Bill. Bill rarely spoke and wouldn't respond to most questions, but he did tell me once that he was a Navy veteran. I've found that the older, mostly male dementia patients, if they can speak at all, are usually able to tell you which branch of the service they served in.

I played every two weeks in Bill's small group home for about a year. One day about four to six months after I stopped doing these gigs, I got a call from a hospice organization; the caller asked if I was the same guy who had played at that facility. Bill was in hospice care now, and he had asked for me by name. A hospice volunteer had tracked down my phone number. I was able to play some songs for Bill that evening in his hospital room, and he passed peacefully later that evening. Being able to be there for him was one of my life's greatest gifts.

On another occasion, at one point during my show, a woman stood up from her wheelchair and raised her hands in the air as if conducting, while simultaneously doing some simple, graceful dance moves. I didn't know her condition well enough to be surprised by this, but I noticed two staff members did seem surprised.

After the show, these staffers told me that Muriel never stood up on her own; she needed help to even get into her wheelchair from her bed.

The mind, in dementia, still has capacities that we don't understand. Even patients who seem "gone" in most observable ways are not beyond the reach of music.

Loving intention and faith—and some well-chosen oldie songs—can create profound healing.

Ron Thomas

THE GREAT PYRAMID
SOUND DOWNLOAD

O n a trip to Egypt, the group I was with booked the Great Pyramid overnight. While in the pyramid, I heard a thundering voice. He announced himself as Archangel Gabriel.

"Seven is the sacred number," he said. "Color, light, sound. Seven is the sacred number." He repeated this over and over.

I wondered if he was talking about the chakras, the seven rays, or the colors of the rainbow, with an activation tone for each chakra. I became so excited about the information that I wanted to go home immediately and compose a chakra sound-activation CD.

But I also thought, *What, am I crazy? I am in the most unbelievable place in the world, the magical land of Egypt!*

I kept thinking about the sacred message and information I had just received. I could not sleep.

I thought, *Okay, I understand what Gabriel meant. There is a musical key and color for each of the seven chakras.*

I put all the information together in my head to develop the chakra-opening CD. I remembered that, on the flight to Egypt, I had wanted to create a CD with the word "journey" in it. *That's it! Chakra Journey!* At that time, I didn't know of any chakra CD's.

When I returned home from Egypt I researched and tested the musical notes to activate each chakra. I went through thousands of sounds on my keyboard before I found the right ones. I recorded the root chakra—but as soon as I started to record the sacral chakra, Archangel Gabriel came in and said, *Not yet!*

"But I am so excited about this project, and I have all the information," I argued.

Not yet, the voice said again.

I tried to keep recording but found that nothing worked in my recording studio.

Every six months, I would try to record the Chakra Journey CD, but I was stopped by Archangel Gabriel's voice every time. He would say, *Not yet.* This went on for four frustrating years. I recorded three other CDs in that period, and everything worked fine for them.

On September 11, 2001, the Twin Towers fell in New York City.

The next day, Archangel Gabriel came in and said, *Okay, it is time now.*

I knew exactly what he meant. I started recording immediately. This time, everything worked. I added the specific tones for each chakra, and the project flowed smoothly.

I now realize why the archangel stopped me for all those years. There is a certain time when things need to happen. My CD for healing and awakening was released exactly at the time it was most needed.

Devara ThunderBeat

INITIATION AT ESALEN

*W*e'd hiked into the Valley of Esalen a few hours before, hearing the duff make soft, crunching sounds under our feet. This valley was filled with the echoes across time of the Esselen peoples who had pilgrimaged there to perform ceremonies. I was humbled and honored to have the opportunity to pray on this blessed land.

Exploring the valley also meant confronting the issues of power and privilege that allowed us to be here. I was determined to do my best, in alignment and in integrity, to continue to honor this land and the generations who had come before.

I also contemplated the lineage holders of transpersonal psychology, depth work, and experiential transformation. My teachers who came before me had made it possible for me to be here at Esalen, to share our gifts and carry the torch of spiritual emergence and extraordinary experiences.

Beyond the drums and chanting that I heard through the Akasha, I began to hear voices in many other languages, sacred songs of prayer from all over the world.

We gathered in the forest classroom and held our ceremony. It was an honoring, an invocation, and a call for the protection of our work. We asked for blessings on our journeys, both collectively, as a field of energy—as a *sangha*—and individually. We dedicated our practice to the benefit of all beings.

Then we searched for places to meditate, to go inward. Some walked or visited the river. We went wherever each of us was called to go.

I felt drawn to a baby redwood tree. A little indentation under a bush near the tree looked like it had been dug out intentionally, at some point, by an animal. It was the perfect size for me to curl up into a fetal position, under my blanket, and go into my meditation. I felt the energy moving through me from my spiritual guides and helpers, healing the places within me that were traumatized and opening formerly blocked channels within my energy body.

These spirit guides told me my body was a sensitive instrument, and that I should care for it like a delicate and powerful tool.

After what seemed like days, but was probably only hours, I began to open my eyes and emerge from my chrysalis. I saw a friend and opened my mouth to ask how they were. The most pristine overtones came through my voice.

The sound was unlike anything I had ever heard before, and I was not in control of it. I could not, and would not want to, stop it. The tones were channeling through me, and with every word I said, they transmitted the most clear, refined healing energy.

For the next several hours, everyone I came into contact with heard these tones in my voice and was impacted by them. For some, it had a clearing/detoxifying effect. For others, the tones were nourishing and soothing. It was as if the sound of my voice became exactly what each person needed.

Even as we closed the ceremony and hiked out of the valley, back toward the lodge, I felt clear, energized, open, and supported by this gift of internal sound healing and the opportunity to share it with others.

Michelle Anne Hobart

THE RHYTHM AND THE KEY

lthough the story was familiar, today the physician's words had the most painful reverberation: "I'm sorry; this pregnancy is not viable. The heartbeat is not strong enough to sustain life. You will begin to miscarry in a few days."

I had delivered one child before with no complications. The doctors had no explanation for my inability to have another.

I was on my way home, to wait for my body to proceed according to its natural course. It was going to be tough, sad, and disheartening to have to explain that it had happened again. It would be hard to feel these sensations of loss and exhaustion again. At times, the grief was unbearable.

Feeling its sacredness, I wanted to honor the little heartbeat inside of my body. I decided to purchase a small drum at a local music shop. It was nothing impressive: small, used, and scratched, but with graphics that reflected sanctity. As I touched its battered sides and held it in my hand, I connected with the drum in a profound way. I knew it was the perfect instrument to orchestrate a nurturing rhythm for my desperate body. Its tone was perfect for my aching heart.

The first little thump was all I needed to feel an inner peace throughout my being. Thump! thump! I lightly tapped. I put the drum close to my heart for no specific reason and without any particular expectation. Thump! thump! thump! The skin of my hands became immersed in this new sensation, a fully embodied experience.

The sound soon became one with me and, within the rhythm, I found a silence I had never known. All mind and matter disappeared as my body merged with the drum's distinctive tone.

As I breathed, I noticed the stillness of my mind. This silence connected instantly to an image in my head that seemed profound and mysterious. It was a picture of a key—a brilliant, vivid, golden, spinning key that moved and spiraled in a dancelike wave. Its dance was intriguing and healing.

Some days, I lay on my side, playing the drum slowly and gently, and as I played, the key introduced other elements and told a story. Although I was not certain of the message, I knew the key held mystical meaning about my loss and miscarriages. Something subtle was happening. My connection to the key and its messages became stronger than my connection to the fetus.

I knew, in this powerful moment of sound, that I was beginning to weaken my attachment to grief and loss, and to hold onto the regenerative, "energetic" state that the sound and key were providing. With the drumming, the key presented a pattern that established a new reference point. This point brought clarity, release, and Divine communication.

A lightness filled my body. I was pregnant and one with the fetus and its spirit, even though I knew we were about to experience separation. I had begun to let go. The sound exuded sincere love and utter surrender. There in the unknown, with the elixir of sound and fascination, I became one with the void. My body was fine. I knew I was connected to something far beyond anything my mind could discern.

The sound of the drum and the essence of the key supported a higher vibration than that of loss, or the mind's definition of loss, or the ego's perception of loss. The rhythm offered complete acceptance of this tiny heart, devoid of a confirming experience.

I continued to drum through the loss; I held tightly to the vision of the key for hope, and I continued to pray for knowledge beyond what my mind considered imaginable. The sacred beat of the drum offered insight and belief that there were deeper, larger meanings—and that I needed patience and trust. To say it simply, this was where Divine timing had met Divine listening.

My drum helped give me the patience I needed; it tapped into my heart's deepest places, places that otherwise could not be touched. The sound allowed for a soft, fluid, glowing connection. I had the capacity to float, to escape time and reality, and to breathe with bliss and peace.

In that space, my grief was non-existent. The drum reintroduced me to vibrations of quintessential openness and harmonized joy. Its heartbeat was the perfect gift to help lift me from the heaviness of earthly matters, the need for possessions, and my expectations.

During these heartbreaking days, the drum's tone, pitch, and melody answered my prayers and gave me insight in the most direct way.

Tamara Knox

OUR WORK WITH THE
MUSIC OF THE PLANTS

*T*here was a story we once read in the book called *Prelude to the Landing on Planet Earth* by Stuart Holroyd that fueled our interest in the plant kingdom's ability to sense emotion, respond to psychic impulses, and be bio-transducers of energy.

In the story a person positioned a plant on a stage in front of skeptics, scientists, and parapsychologists to elicit a healing response through the plant via an osmosis effect. Basically, they used the plant as a transducer to send healing vibrations into the audience, and the response was literally "electrifying."

As musicians/composers who play electronic concerts, we created a show called "Supersensonics," where we brought a potted plant on stage in an attempt to duplicate what was demonstrated with the osmosis effect. As the performance commenced, the first thing the audience experienced was a pre-programmed visual code 11:11 which began to flash 11 times—the text on the screen was cinema size in height. Then the performance continued as we started to play live sacred ambient music.

A plant around two feet in height was sitting on the front of the stage, ready to respond to our music. The plant was spotlighted with a down spotlight, ready to transmit energies of the music into the audience as healing tones. Most of the audience wasn't necessary spiritual but was open to this sacred music performance. We all played together for over an hour, weaving New Age music from ourselves and various composers, coupled with cosmic synths, harmonic toning, and Tibetan bowls. It made for a deeply meditative performance.

After the concert, we chatted with some audience members to gauge their responses. One woman sitting in our group looked considerably shaken, but calm. She said that, as the 11:11 flashed, her deceased mother appeared to her and talked to her through her mind. Now, she didn't really believe in such things, but the experience was so real that she burst into tears.

We thought this experience was interesting and felt that the plant may have helped to transmit the energy during our show. We decided to have the plant accompany us for more live performances. Each time, we were fascinated by the experiences that audience members would report.

It was clear to us that plants could transmit energy. This began our journey into the "music of the plants." We asked ourselves, "If plants could speak? What would they say?"

A few years later, we performed in a new theater space called the "Ascension Engine" in Melbourne, Australia. It was there that a member of the Damanhur Community came to speak about the music of the plants and how plants could sing when hooked up to an electronic device. They literally communicated via sound—actual audible frequencies.

After meeting the presenter from Damanhur, we realized that, to move our show to the next level with plants who could sing, we must make similar devices. This allowed us to hook up many plants at the local botanical gardens and create performances that were literally musical symphonies from the plants.

The paranormal idea that plants can communicate or even have a certain nervous/brain system was becoming known, and in recent years, plant researchers have found that plants also have memory. We find now that the science complements the spiritual reality of human-plant communication.

Another experience with the music of the plants occurred one day when we were in the bicentennial conservatory at the Adelaide Botanic Gardens. It was towards the end of the day, and a woman who was pregnant came in.

She said to us, "This is all silly. There is no communication between plants and humans; this is not possible."

We then witnessed, as she walked along the garden path towards our device, that the plant stopped singing! As she moved further away, it started up again. While this plant had its own pattern of plant music, in the eight days we had been there, it had never exhibited this type of behavior.

As she walked back towards us, it stopped singing again. Now she came up to us amused and asked how this was possible. We explained that just as humans have electromagnetic fields, plants do also, and there is a constant interaction and biofeedback between living systems. As she preceded to walk by the plant again and attempt to touch it, it stopped making sound again.

Experiences like these, and many others, encouraged us to delve deeper into larger installations and art exhibitions of the music of the plants. We feel that through these experiences, audience members gain a deeper appreciation and understanding of their symbiotic relationship with nature and the positive impact they can have through respecting, not destroying, nature. Ultimately, we feel we are to share love powered emanations with all of the natural kingdom as caretakers of our place in the universe.

From the Findhorn community to other eco-communities of Europe, it is said that the nature spirits want a voice; they want to be heard, and this is what happened in 2022. After one of our major musical events that took place over nine nights, we felt there was presence around our musical space. That evening, turning off the lights, we talked to each other about the profound energy shift in the space and that nature felt happy. Right at that moment, I (Darren), and another witness, saw a small glowing sphere of light rise from the bottom of the floor in front of our faces in a sparkling luminesce of radiant glow; it looked like a fairy. Just in a flash, before our eyes, it vanished. We looked at each other in bewilderment, checking that we had seen the same thing. On confirmation, we felt that this was the greatest success of the show, that nature had responded, and the spiritual dimensions manifested to us.

Working with plants brings us great joy and pushes us into new musical environments as we seek to help people reconnect with their inner and outer nature and to experience the sounds of the cosmos.

The great work we are now concentrating on is called "Axiatonal Music" which considers the human body as the prime musical instrument. Here we entertain the background sound patterns of the universe in sync with the acupuncture system of the body as illustrated by Dr. J.J. Hurtak in *The Keys of Enoch*®. The result is a higher synthesis of bio-music, sound and psycho-energetic healing patterns which create a marvelous soundscape in the inner musical temple of the body.

Darren Curtis and Bradley Pitt

SOUND IN THE GREAT PYRAMID

s professional archaeologists and explorers, we went to Egypt on numerous occasions in the 1980s and 1990s. J.J. had taught, amongst other topics, musical bio-feedback in collaboration with his colleagues, Morton Subotnik and also Nam June Paik, the founder of video art, in the faculty of California Institute of the Arts, and Desiree had studied environmental design and architecture. Having both studied music and being aware of the frequency resonances and their effects on the body, we knew the importance of sound in sacred spaces and wanted to test the musical sound patterns within the Great Pyramid. We felt that there was a pyramidal energy field that generated a type of acoustical physics within the design of the pyramid that could be tapped.

It is not just about finding hidden rooms but working within the pyramid to activate its latent powers to become as an energy vehicle, even a beacon of Light. In short, we believe that the Great Pyramid was designed as a vibratory temple of learning, healing, and meditation, and then also as a place for energy technology as well as global and astrophysical communication using sound. With the perfect geometry, everything is possible!

We had previously been on official expeditions on the Giza Plateau using ground penetrating radar, but our search for a deeper understanding of sound resonance continued to haunt us. In 2006, we were in Egypt to continue our musical testing, this time with Alan Howarth and others who had a background in music and technology, as we wanted to test the reality of the acoustical properties of each of the known rooms using the most modern equipment. Our testing involved sending out pink and white noise electronic sweeps into the chambers, and also using human voices. After several minutes of vocalization, we were able to enter into a higher state of consciousness and began to discern one of the deep and profound experiences connected with our perception of a vibratory "Language of Light" as spoken of in *The Keys of Enoch*® that could open and convey a stream of consciousness from a higher level of universal knowledge.

We were taking pictures at the same time, and at one point in the King's Chamber near the sarcophagus, our strong musical vocalizations caused large phenomena, commonly called "orbs," to appear out of the vibratory background. Three mandala like orbs were clearly seen in the photographs. Their floating designs exhibited patterns of circles and unique geometries within the circles. We took several pictures and were able to watch the pattern of orbs encircle the open coffer. Was this an ancient Egyptian tomb or was it a sacred energy resonator with star alignments that could reach to the famous regions of Orion and the star Sirius?

After a period in which pictures were taken of the orb apparitions, we went into an even deeper state of prayer and meditation using Sacred Names. On an earlier expedition, while in the King's Chamber, Desiree was verbalizing sacred mantra sounds and felt that the "sides" of the King's Chamber opened up completely on all sides, and she was sitting in outer space as if the chamber itself had become transparent. The entire chamber became an active place for not only initiation but also expanded super-consciousness whereby the human body could be suddenly lifted into space.

Desiree later heard that this experience was similar to that of a mutual friend, Dr. Robert Sundar Dreyfus, while he was also in the King's Chamber. Later, on a Gaia TV program called *Deep Space* in the episode titled *Energy Secrets of the Great Pyramid*, one of the people interviewed had a very similar experience where the "walls fell away" and the stars of the night sky could be experienced! This type of experience seems to allow the human initiate as a musical being to momentarily become a *cosmocrator* (Greek), a prime subject who orchestrates his consciousness by self-realization of integrated beauty and sound, taking a higher path of dedication.

In Egypt, a prime symbol is the pyramid form that in Greek means "Fire in the Middle." The King's Chamber could be an initiation chamber to teach people to find their higher consciousness through energizing the human body as a musical-instrument, activating the energies of the temple. Perhaps, most importantly, this gives us an understanding of who we really are on earth and in the cosmos.

Many people have come to the Great Pyramid and sounded ancient expressions, aiding in the process of understanding our place in the cosmos. This confirms what we believe—in singing Sacred Names, we tap into a paraphysical energy life force that was recognized by the ancients.

On an earlier occasion, our singer-associate, Paul Thomas Burns, who was living in Egypt at the time, was with us in the Great Pyramid, and as we began to vocalize ancient mantras in the Grand Gallery, we began to see sound correlations as our voices became stronger and stronger. Suddenly, before our eyes, streaks of white and yellow light began to manifest— cascading down from some unknown source into the interior of the gallery. We could see these lights without having to take pictures, but when we did take a picture, it seemed that the entire room was lit up. Literally, the entire Grand Gallery was filled with an unusual light, and we were able to capture it with our camera.

Some readers may be familiar with the story of the ancient people of God living in Egypt, or the reference to Moses in the New Testament *Book of Acts 7:22*, which says, "Moses had all of the wisdom of Egypt, he was powerful in words and deeds..." suggesting that there was once an interplay between sacred Hebrew and Egyptian teachings by those who were in service to the guardianship and preservation of teachings on the Great Pyramid. Our linguistic background allowed both of us, as a great mystery associated with sounds and music was unveiled, to understand the cymatic energy patterns of combined sounds and mantras.

In retrospect, the sound events, we believe, helped to create remarkable signs and wonders, enabling us to see how some forms of sacred language (labials, syllables, gutturals, etc.), when invoked, could produce something so wonderful and overpowering that it seems that a dimensional doorway is being opened through sound. Today, we understand this as a "paraphysical sign" given to both of us to understand our contemporary role in Egypt and provide a momentary glimpse into our future work from an earlier experience that would lead us into the use of breathing and song to create a unique acoustical physics through sacred musical linguistics to activate ancient places of initiation.

Drs. J. J. and Desiree Hurtak

PART THREE

Deepening Your Experience with Sound

We listen to music with our muscles.

— FRIEDRICH NIETZSCHE

MEDITATIVE QUALITIES OF SOUND

*W*hen we meditate, we often concentrate all our mental and emotional energy within us, and that works well for clearing and calming the mind. Another method of meditation is not only to go "within" but also simultaneously to connect "without."

Why would we send and receive energies outside of ourselves while in a state of meditation? Because we are not alone in the universe, and we need to connect to our higher selves, as well as to bring that energy into who we are, here and now. Also, when we ourselves become harmonized, we can send that energy out to help humanity and the world around us.

Realizing also that everything in life is vibration, we have come to know that we are all not vibrating on the same note. Nevertheless, we can still see each of us as parts of a greater symphony of Creation. We sometimes create clashing sounds, but then we know we need to shift to a more harmonious melody. Whether we look at nature outside of ourselves or go into our inner nature, we realize that we are all emanating fields which should be focused into dynamic harmonies of Love and Joy.

So, when we emanate our energies, we are also able to say and sing sacred vibrations, composed of Sacred Names, Sacred Thought as Expressions, and

Sacred Vibrations. It is our understanding that these emanations go beyond the locality of the room or outdoor space we may be sitting in and, in fact, can be heard in the heavens.

SACRED GEOMETRY MEDITATION

We see the beauty of nature in all of Life, in the water, in the sounds of the waves and in the singing of the chorus of Humanity. We see within the geometries, the matrix of the Earth that we are all dancing within. The various colors of the rainbow come into our view, and we witness our connection with all the geometries and colors of the chakras.

Now let us add to this, the sacred sounds connected with the seven chakra centers of our body, or seal in the biblical tradition, as we correlate the geometries of each chakra to the traditional sounds given by the ancient Sanskrit sages.

The **First Chakra**, *Muladhara* (base of spine), is equated with the *Bhurloka* of the Earth, where the body is grounded to the earth. This allows us to have a feeling of stability and appreciation of our place on the Earth, here and now.

The symbol traditionally is the triangle pointing downwards to the earth, the place of your incarnation, surrounded by a square, the location of our reality with the four cardinal points, surrounded by the circle for our planet but also for ongoing life, as the word chakra means "wheel" which can be represented by the circle. Even the circle can be expanded as seen in the petals of the flower, usually four, that extend out around the chakra like a blossoming flower. The color of the symbol is red. The traditional mantra is LAM; let us say it 12 times:

LAM (12X)

The **Second Chakra**, *Svadhisthana* (below the navel), is considered an energy associated with *Bhuvarloka*. While still connected to the energies of the earth and the sun, it has a way of creating and establishing our place in the reality of Life. Although it is associated with emotions and passion, that energy can be transformed into creative positive energy that flows through us.

The symbol appears as a series of circles, usually three, with an overlapping of each one aligning towards the bottom so that the middle one looks somewhat like a crescent or moon shape. These three together are surrounded also by the petals of a flower, usually eight. The color of the symbol is orange. The mantra is:

VAM (12X)

The **Third Chakra**, *Manipura* (solar plexus), is connected with the sun (and all its planets) as detailed by *Svarloka*, as the solar plexus harmonizes with the "fire" of the sun. So, the energy here is associated with "light energy" that is both in the body but also surrounding the body and helps to continue our life force and to bring forth a higher consciousness into the physical world.

Again, in the center is the triangle pointing downwards to the earth—but this time there is no square around it, and its edges touch the outer circle. The circle is surrounded by eight petals for the movement connecting the sun to the greater suns in the heavens, the stars and that which is beyond. The color of the symbol is yellow. The mantra is:

RAM (12X)

The **Fourth Chakra**, *Anahata* (heart chakra), is where the Divine Energy truly begins to open within the body, establishing a higher body of Loving Harmony, expanding consciousness to the *Maharloka*, which reveals the opening of the universe, even beyond the local stars. So, the heart not only opens us up to appreciate the fuller universe we live in, but it is also the inner temple that radiates the Love for all Creation.

Here, the symbol is two intersecting triangles like the Hebrew star of David which shows us how we need to receive the energies of the heavens but also balance it with the heart as we also connect to the earth we live on. It is surrounded by a circle but has 12 petals of the flower around it. The color of the symbol is green. The mantra is:

YAM (12X)

The **Fifth Chakra**, *Vishuddha* (throat chakra), moves us to the point that our Love becomes an Inspiration. It corresponds to *Janaloka*, where the beings who live in this consciousness reality have control over the elements of nature. That control comes through sound and frequencies that are able to heal and transform the cells of our body, but also help to awaken those around us through the voice of Love, Peace, and Understanding.

So, the symbol is the central triangle pointing down to the earth with each of its three vertices touching the circle, as the voice is that which also helps to brings the energy of the heavens to the earth. However, the corners of each of the three sides of the triangle complexifies to create a six-sided inner geometry of a hexagon. So, at the inner side is a hexagon that expands to become a downward pointing triangle surrounded by a circle with 18 petals of the flower around it. The color of the symbol is aquamarine blue. The mantra is:

HAM (12X)

The **Sixth Chakra**, *Ajna* (third eye), opens us to Divine Insight connected also with the powers of the *Tapoloka* associated with the Knowledge realms.

This is the opening of the third eye and is the only real geometry that is elongated to the right and left side just as the third eye is placed between the top of your head and your two eyes. This is truly the beginning of insights that are beyond what our five senses can reveal. We see how time and space become illusory when we can bear witness to a greater reality of knowing: past, present, and future.

It again has a triangle in the center pointing downwards, the corners of the triangle touching the circle. Yet, around the circle are only two petals which reach out to the left and right side of the circle—symbolic of the opening of all eyes to higher wisdom and Light. The color of the symbol is indigo. The seed mantra is "OM," but one can add the supernal sound of:

PRANAVA – OM (12X)
(SANSKRIT: THE COSMIC SOUND)

The **Seventh Chakra**, *Sahasrara* (*Kether*, Crown Chakra), brings us into Godliness and the Experience of the *Satyaloka* (or *Brahmaloka*), the realm where the heavenly holarchies, the angelic beings, reside. It is they who give us the "overview" from a reality that is All-Knowing, All-Loving, and All-Caring.

The symbol is truly the many-petaled lotus flower unfolding, but at the heart is the circle which then has several tiers of blossoms around it—the blossoms are now in layers upon layers, as many layers as you would imagine for the dimensions or worlds that are required to reach into the higher heavens. The color of the symbol is violet. The seed mantra is "OM," or some say "AUM," as we align all seven chakras with the power of:

OM (12X)

DIVINE MIND MEDITATION

We go within and visualize the temple of the Spirit inside of us. We hear our heartbeat; we feel our breathing getting slower and slower as we relax and contemplate the vastness and the beauty of Life. Our Consciousness now is aware of the Universal Mind that exists throughout the Universe, and we can tap into all aspects of Life wherever it exists, in the many dimensions, and feel we are One with the greater flow of Life. With this, we find true higher consciousness as we sing:

OM PURNAMADAH PURNAMIDAM (12X)
(SANSKRIT: OM, BEHOLDING THE WHOLE/THE INFINITE/THE PERFECTION, THIS IS THE WHOLE/THE INFINITE/THE PERFECTION)

Our mind dynamics rise to a new level of focus. We feel that Infinite within us as we radiate it out to all the world. This is the Peace that passes all human Understanding. We resonate with that greater Peace and send it with the Power of Love into the Consciousness Field of Life through the power of our Mind linked with the Divine Mind.

MUSIC OF THE PLANTS MEDITATION

Let us sing to the plants, sharing vibrations of Love. We all live on Mother Earth, and it is important that we are consciously aware of the greater Garden of Creation. Let us continue our role as caretakers for the planet in helping all life forms to live, develop, and thrive. Let us strive to hear the music of the plants, as we sing to them the words:

VISHNU GAIA (12X)
(SANSKRIT/GREEK: THE PRESERVER OF EARTH MOTHER)

Let us see ourselves interconnected with all Life forms in the greater Kingdom of Creation.

MUSIC OF THE SPHERES MEDITATION

We look to the stars and understand what the Mayans have told us regarding the one who is the lady cloth weaver of the cosmos. We know that every star is in its proper place in the heavens, placed there by a higher authority, and in turn, we are also in our place to assist with the heavens as we say:

IX ZACAL NUK (12X)
(LADY CLOTH WEAVER, PRONOUNCED "EE ZA-KAL NUK")

We hear the Music of the Spheres singing back to us as the sounds of the stars, the planets and the comets all are in harmony with the Universe.

SOUND HEALING MEDITATION

Much like plants, we can create superior interconnection using sounds and vibrations which bring us together with other forms of intelligence and each other in the greater harmony of Life.

As our body begins to resonate with the power of the sounds of Life, the sounds of Creation, the sounds of the Universe, we cannot hear every sound, but we can resonate with those sounds, as we are all interconnected. The Power of the Sounds begins to heal our bodies, minds, and souls. The very cells within our bodies and our DNA begin to vibrate with the Light, which is from the greater realms of Creation. We call upon the angelic hosts to be with us in our healing process and especially Raphael whose name means to heal:

RAPHA RAPHAEL (12X)
(HEBREW: TO HEAL THROUGH THE ANGEL OF HEALING)

We feel the greater Love surrounding us, like the wings of the angels. There is no end to this Love; it is the Love of the Divine that helps to bring us back into our original State of Divine Beingness with Love, Wisdom, and Understanding.

SACRED TEMPLE MEDITATION

We stand within the Sacred Temple walls, and we realize that the temple is our body. As we evolve through death and cycles of rebirth or, as thought in ancient Egypt, beyond Osiris and Isis, we experience spherical, musical energy field relationships which death has not touched at all. We are the Temple of the Divine Spirit; we are the Temple of Light, the Temple of Understanding. All parts of our body are now harmonized through the mental dynamics within us as we focus our New Being, our Initiated Selves, on the Transformative Story of Creation. The Temple, whether it be the body or the structure of ancient times, now opens to take us into the Greater heavens as the Pharaohs rode on the solar boats to return to the heavens of Orion and beyond. We return to the ancient Egyptian cosmology which understood the heavenly realms but also the power of the Sonship of Horus who appeared both in the heavens and upon the Earth as we sing:

HOREM-AKHET (12X)
(EGYPTIAN: HORUS ON THE HORIZON)

The sky is no longer the limit. There is no limit with our higher consciousness body now initiated into the Light; there is only our greater discovery of the Cosmos and those who indwell within it.

May the Heavenly Temple and the Human Temple come together and reveal the Eternal Voice of the Divine.

Amen.

USING THE SACRED NAMES AND EXPRESSIONS

*A*ccording to Wisdom Literature, the Great Traditions and Movements of Thought, Sacred Expressions (also called Mantras in the East), are part of the Holy Language of Sound that can actively link the human mind to experiences in connection with the Cosmic Intelligence and a state of Oneness with the universe and the Godhead. This is done through sound patterns that, for many, also bring about inspiration, spiritual refreshment, and an inner sanctification of holiness, and for those who seek to activate their participation in a larger reality, it reveals a space that, in many ways, elevates the human mind into higher states of Consciousness.

We mainly exist in a limited 3rd dimensional level of understanding of the world around us, but as our soul evolves and our mind expands, we realize we sometimes can have the ability to see not only into the past and the future, but also other realities. Sometimes, those from other realms are also around, and the Power behind the Names helps us to co-participate with them and to discover these other realities of existence.

Each soul interested in the higher heavenly worlds is given the musical and spiritual training and capacity to work in myriad realms inhabited and controlled by consciousness entities who exist beyond the evolutionary specifics of earth life. So, in addition to improving our memory and cognitive thought, as in the "Mozart Effect," we can also understand the past and anticipate the future by opening the "mind-locks" that have limited us, so we can enter into higher evolutionary dimensions.

We encourage everyone to use the Sacred Names and Expressions also for protection, as the Names are as shields of energy defense. So, the one who is calling forth a higher energy field receives that protection. Therefore, when we are strong in the Names of God, we are also inspired and less threatened by events taking place around us. The Divine Godhead responds to our prayers personally, not just with Love, but in ways that can change the reality around us and within us.

The ancient Chinese sutras speak of employing a higher spectrum of super-consciousness to go beyond this three-dimensional reality spectrum and how the soul can be guided on a journey from beginning to end to a new beginning. Thus, the ancients recognized the "Language of Light" which is also considered having musical nodes of quavers (eighth note) and semi-quavers (sixteenth note) that can be used to attain a fuller experience of Life.

Thus, Sacred Chants provide certain musical qualities for human communication interacting with the Masters and Avatars who are beings spoken of in Eastern traditions. In the West, these superluminal realities include the Angelic and Archangelic beings. Here, musical vibrations are deemed essential for higher communication between those in the heavens and those of us in our planetary realm. In modern science, we would describe these higher or superluminal dimensions of meta-creation as having a greater understanding of Life. So, our spirit is able to use paraphysics and music for the soul's evolutionary soundscape into a greater reality of Life.

In this meditation, we will use the vibrational sounds of the Hebrew-Aramaic, Greek-Coptic, Sanskrit-Tibetan, and Egyptian Languages as examples of communication tools with the Divine Mind. In a "subtle musical" way, the Sacred Names and Expressions from many ancient languages are as a living energy that can bring us into new levels of communication. We affirm that the sounds behind these ancient Names and Expressions will not only help to unify the left and right hemispheres of the human brain, but also can become as a cosmic telephone line to greater dimensions of Awareness. The vibrations literally work to bridge the gap between the Divine and all life forms living in the Garden of Life, as well as to prepare our Soul to discover a greater enhanced awareness.

LET OUR MEDITATION BEGIN!

With the Sacred Powers of Sound and Light, we first journey "within" to transform our body, mind, and soul. We seek to find that inner peace that passes all human understanding. We have been sensitized to hear the musical vibrations taking place around us and within us, which helps us now to move our mind into harmony with the purification of Light that is also taking place in all aspects of our being.

We feel our heart and "third eye" align and come into perfect balance as our soul begins to advance to new levels of experience. Our body now is generating beautiful musical healing geometries within us, and we begin to witness the harmonics of a Higher Presence, our Overself body, beginning to become manifest within our embodiment of flesh. We listen to our heartbeat that sings to us a message of Peace in Sanskrit as:

OM, SHANTI, SHANTI, SHANTI (12X)
(SANSKRIT: OM, PEACE, PEACE, PEACE)

We feel the Power of the OM resonating throughout our body. Whether we sing it aloud or we vibrate it within us so no one hears, it places us into a greater sense of harmonious balance, felt and experienced by the heart, mind, and soul. Our entire body begins to resonate and transform itself. We now know that we are part of the "Music of the Spheres," as every cell in our body comes into perfect harmony within the universe, and there is really no separation between the "me" and the "we"—all is One. We acknowledge the ancient tantras that reveal how all creation can be seen as the manifestation of a Supreme Unbounded Consciousness. With this, we vibrate within us, as well as sing out loud:

OM MANI PADME HUM (12X)
(SANSKRIT: PRAISE TO THE JEWEL IN THE LOTUS)

As we are one with the Universe, we really have no limitations, and so we soar above this world, and as we do, we look down and see the temples of the world. One of these temple areas looks like the Great Pyramid of Egypt with beams of subtle light energy radiating out from it. Music also comes upwards and outwards from its tetrahedral center; in fact, we can also see myriads of colors. We inwardly know that we are seeing multi-color ionization that is in harmony with all the musical tones and vibrations of the other energy grids or vortex points of the planet.

We are being drawn downwards towards the Great Pyramid and are able to hear, once again, the ancient voices of those who had been singing in the temples and calling out to the Divine Mother. Yet, we hear not the names of Isis nor Nephthys, her sister, as we would expect, but we hear the name of:

MA'AT (12X)
(EGYPTIAN: [COSMIC] MOTHER)

Ma'at is the power of Creation and the thoughts behind the Cosmic Order, who brings balance and harmony to Life. Her masculine counterpart is known as Thoth, the scribe. Now we see ourselves as part of a greater Divine

Family with myriads upon myriads of spiritual beings who attend to the workings of the universe. With the knowledge of the Divine Feminine, we see her manifestation in all Life forms. As we paraphysically enter into the Great Pyramid, we, too, resonate her Name as the sound frequencies move into powerful musical harmonic vibrations. These vibrations are so strong that her creative presence seems to be able to bring the dead back to life.

From Egypt, we travel East, and we come to the area of Jerusalem, another powerful vortex point in the Middle East. Moving around the Holy Land, we continue to hear prayers of praise to the Trinity Powers; yet, in all the songs and praises, what stands out is the Name for the "Presence of the Godhead" known as the *Shekinah*. Let us use this vibration as we know it also has the "She" representing the feminine part of the Godhead as an integral part of its vibrations as we say:

SHEKINAH (12X)
(HEBREW: PRESENCE OF GOD)

We wish to exalt You, O Divine Mother, in all places around the world. Your Grace and Glory radiate through all Your multiple manifestations to all peoples. As we sing, we begin to feel the vibrations that are sung in the superluminal realms of the Angels and Archangels and the Avatars and Maha-Avatars of the Eastern tradition.

As we begin to sing also special sounds of praise which, we know, are essential for higher communication with those in the heavens, we begin to resonate a heavenly musical vibration within ourselves. We are told in all sacred Scriptures that in the temples there were the sounds of trumpets, harps, timbales, stringed instruments, and sometimes loud cymbals. With this as our background, we too sing with the angels as we say:

SANCTUS, SANCTUS, SANCTUS (12X)
(LATIN: HOLY, HOLY, HOLY)

This Expression is sung by the Seraphim angels, and so before we continue with our journey connected with the Divine Mother, we first enhance within us the musical harmonics to open up the powers of our mind and call upon the Divine Hosts of Light. These are all gifts given to us from the Cosmic Brotherhoods and Sisterhoods of Light connected with the Ophanim, the Cherubim, and the Seraphim, as well as the other Lords of Light from above who are still waiting for us to sing or say the sacred mantras, the sacred words to call upon the Most High.

As we manifest a richness within through sounds, we begin to find an inner peace and joy through the vibrations of music and the rhythms of shared Life in concert with all those who dwell in the Heavenly worlds. These include the invisible realms of the Divine Spirit working through the endowments of vibrations and songs of thanksgiving. Together, with the sovereignty of the Divine Spirit, we mount up to a higher state of Consciousness to sing with the angelic beings who lead the human soul from material existence to the non-material realms and into greater dimensions of Life. Again, we are in perfect resonance with the true "Music of the Spheres" which is more than the position of the planets, it is the very harmony of the universe.

O Divine Hosts of Light, may Your Names reside within us, and bless and guide us as we witness the coming of those beings called the "Ultimate Triumphants" as we behold the myriads of beings in the heavens and so we acknowledge this reality as we say:

BASILEIA TOU THEOU (12X)
(GREEK: KINGDOM OF GOD)

In the midst of the Heavenly Kingdom, we see Cities of Light, and as we come closer, we see how each city is composed of Sacred Geometries and variations of Light. Within the cities are glowing Light beings that inhabit them, and surrounding it are gigantic wheels within wheels that have been built to travel throughout the galaxies and myriad universes that exist. We are told the sacred wheeled vehicles are called the *Merkabah*, and each soul interested in the higher heavenly journey can enter within them, when we are gifted with the musical and spiritual training and the consciousness capacity to work in myriad realms. Now we know, these realms are inhabited by consciousness entities who exist beyond the evolutionary specifics of our earthly life, yet they have given us certain musical qualities of communication, allowing us to commune with them.

And so, we begin to understand the power of the thought-forms that have created the "House of Many Mansions" as we are introduced to the vastness of creation having not only many planets and evolutionary possibilities of life, but also the many different transitional realms beyond the stellar regions. We now know that all is created by means of musical vibrations and Divine Thought. Each vibration allows the human soul to live in different principalities and paradises. Now, we understand how we are part of a greater Treasury of Light that the Coptic Christians spoke of, as we proclaim:

THESAUROS PHOS (12X)
(GREEK: TREASURY OF LIGHT)

O Father of all fatherhoods, Mother of all motherhoods, Source of Sources, Light of all Lights, receive our prayers of sacred vibrations in service to all humanity. Using Your Holy Names and Sacred Expressions to call upon the greater Light, we comprehend the vastness of Your Glory flowing into our heart that begins to synergize songs and hymns of Ascension. Through our sounds, we behold the awakening of a new humanity that shares the evolutionary process of Light and Love in all possible realities.

Now we move to the East to China and hear the reading aloud of the ancient Chinese sutras that speak of employing a higher spectrum of super-consciousness. The ancient sutras have shown many devoted pilgrims how to go beyond our electromagnetic spectrum, as they guide the journey of the soul from beginning to end to new beginning. We now recognize how the fuller experience of the Buddha allowed the human soul to pass through the gross material universe into the brighter Consciousness Universe of Light and "overtone" sounds, as we hear and see how "all things can be made anew" according to the Infinite Way!

The Holy Sutras give us the chants/prayers to sing to help align our consciousness to find inner peace, inner joy, and a greater inner Understanding that leads us to our Awakening. The Buddha's words and vibrations resound in our hearts, as we behold also the Divine Lady Kwan Yin sitting herself upon a mountain peak. She has many arms with which she reaches out to the world and especially those who call her Name. She shows them great compassion, and so we, too, call upon her:

KWAN YIN (12X)
(CHINESE: MOTHER OF COMPASSION)

We know the Buddha taught during his lifetime that this planet was an important place for soul growth and that there is work we all have to do on the inner and outer levels in each of our lives. We are all to be servants to humanity as he was a great Teacher and Servant.

Next, we journey into the Great Himalayas and the region of Tibet. We see around us the great temples that reach into the clouds, but as we approach them, we also hear the Name of:

YUM-CHEN-MO (12X)
(TIBETAN: MOTHER OF WISDOM/PERFECTION)

She awakens the deeper vibrations of sound within us, and we ourselves begin to take quantum-jumps through different frequencies that connect with every chakra of our body, moving us out of the individual reality into new collective reality and connecting us with sounds of the myriad other dimensions. Once again, we perceive how the human mind in higher states of consciousness has the ability to connect with Light entities using acoustical wave patterns that help us move into the cosmic matrix of the universe revealing a greater power of Creative energy.

We soar now to India to continue our understanding of the power of the Divine Mother, the Mother of not just our outer universe, but the Inner Path of Divine Creativity. Her Names are on our lips as we look to experience and bless the sacred places of humanity with these Holy Names. Now in India, we proclaim her as we say:

ADI SHAKTI (12X)
(SANSKRIT: PRIMORDIAL CREATIVE POWER)

She has the power, not just of the Earthly Mother, but of the Divine Mother who is behind the Creative Power of Life, in alignment with what many cultures call the Divine Father—although in the heavens all is One. Yet, we exist in a realm of duality, and so we require the Knowledge of the two to be in perfect harmony, like the need to merge the two hemispheres of our brain or the two hemispheres of the planet.

So, although there are many other places we can visit, we feel the call to travel to the mountains of the Andes in South America in the Western Hemisphere, and when we arrive, we see the ancient sacred temples of Machu Pichu as well as Tiahuanaco near the sacred Lake Titicaca. These are temples that have long been deserted, but one can still hear the music of the ancient Inca and pre-Inca peoples who called out to the Divine Mother to help them. Now we chant and vibrate along with them:

PACHAMAMA (12X)
(QUECHUA: EARTH MOTHER)

She helps us to realize we can also control the elements of nature through the musical vibrations of Light. This was already known to the Indigenous peoples, as seen in the Rain Dance that could manifest and change the natural elements as needed. So, we acknowledge You, O Mother of the Earth who aligns with the Mother of the Heavens. You nourish us with Your sanctified sounds as we affirm Your Healing Presence through Your many Names—Shanti, Shanti, Shekinah, Shekinah, Shakti, Shakti—that take us forward with greater Compassion and power of co-creativity. Let these Names help us to activate more of our Life's purpose through inner joy and loving-kindness so we can share more of Your Unconditional Love with others and be strengthened in our Soul-Spirit.

We know the Language of Light is composed of music and sacred geometry that dawns upon us from all directions as our awakened bodies and minds are able to share in becoming Awakened humanity with a greater spirituality of Love. We now have experienced the ever-present Divine Consciousness within and without, and so, we have gained the courage to be more Loving and Creative in working with the myriad combinations of colors and sounds. We now see empowering and healing sacred geometries in all of Life. In seeing and using the holistic dimensions of Creation, we stand upon the sacred ground as *Christopheroi*, Christ-bearers, so we, too, can help provide humanity with "future knowledge" of the Divine Family in the Heavens meeting our Family upon the Earth. Let us never stop seeking the Light and understanding the Power of the Word as sound while we proclaim:

LOGOS THEOU (12X)
(GREEK: WORD OF THE DIVINE)

We know that we are all Christ-bearers when we use the sacred vibrations of sound and music associated with the prophets, the sages, the apostles, the mystics and poets, and the Buddha and Bodhisattvas who shared with us in the Language of Light. As experiencers of sacred sounds, we become witnesses to the Wisdom of the "presence of Higher Life." We are also given the insights to help each person make a momentary "leap of faith" in graduating beyond the veil of three-dimensional life into an incorruptible body of Light energy. Again, we recognize that all life is vibrations, and when we resonate with the right vibrations, we find a level of Peace that is transformational! With this, let us bring the Spirit of Peace throughout the universe as we unify the East and West together and say:

OM SHALOM (12X)
(SANSKRIT/HEBREW: THE UNIVERSAL VIBRATION
(WITH) PEACE)

Let us behold our new body that makes use of the paraphysical energy of Light and Love in becoming a "New Being." As long as our thoughts remain pure, that is, centered within the Spirit of God, we can receive the miracle of the renewed Christed nature as our inner transformation is being made ready for our passage from the third dimension into the fifth dimension. We now behold the continuity of life within the greater continuum.

Let us also pray: O Most High, we are Your Sons and Daughters of Light. We accept that You are the Source and the Expression of Life throughout the universe and the multi-universes. You who existed before the dawning of life, before the beginnings of our variable Sun, we can now acknowledge the vastness of our own vibrating Reality!

Although we may be nearing the end of this epoch with the coming partial collapse of our planetary habitat, a new opportunity has come to us to work with Your Names and Expressions that are to be used for miracles through the assistance of the Heavenly Host. We ask You to commence in activating the Spirit of the Holy within us. Your Spirit gives us the power of Love.

We know when Your Names and Expressions are vibrating sound and color, we will raise our arms and eyes and connect with You and our Spiritual Family, including the Brotherhoods and Sisterhoods of Light, and we can do miracles in this life and in the next chapter of Life. There we will completely put on the garment of Your Names that we will use in Eternity.

All Praise to You, O Infinite One, in all Your Names! We praise You as the Way, Truth, and Life—You, who gave us the Truth and Transformation for all people of the Earth to align to Your Divine Light Power and Love as we work with the angelic hierarchies of Light and the Christed Ones. With music and elevated sounds, we will work for the gathering "of the Tribes" as the tribe of Peace and Love. You who bring hope to the Cry of Mother Earth, let our lessons as Earth pilgrims continue through the miracles of prayer and praise in using the vibrations and acoustics of Your Holy Names. We are ready for the work of Ascension as we say:

ANALIPSI STO PHOS (12X)
(GREEK: ASCENSION TO THE LIGHT)

As we see ourselves in Garments of Light, with Peace, sharing Love and having a greater Understanding of our Mission of Life, we close by saying:

Amen, Amen, Amen
and Amen.

In this meditation, we have used sounds to reach out to the Divine Source of all Sources. Through music and sound, our souls have created vibrations that can help to carry us into the Eternal Realms of Life.

We appreciate the blessings we have been given while on the earth, where we have learned through soul growth to work in harmony with all Life in Service to a greater Reality field that we are part of. Now we have begun to see beyond the limitations of our five senses as we have discovered our own being as being in between Being and Becoming. Yes, we have been inwardly led into the higher path by the sounds, so we can sing with the Angels and Archangels, the Masters and Ascended Masters, and the Buddha and Bodhisattvas, as we awaken into the Cosmos with a greater Consciousness of Sacred Sounds, Peace, and Love in our Hearts.

We are also now souls of Light Consciousness that have learned to sing the sound of the OM and the Amen, which have led us to a world without end, a universe without end, and ultimately the House of Many Mansions without end. We have discovered we are immortal Souls of Radiant musical vibrations that will sing throughout the Cosmos—as we have been Blessed.

To listen to the sacred sounds and meditations visit https://sacredstories.com/commonsentience-sound.

THE SACRED SONG OF THE SOUL

*O*ur experience of sound is one of the keys to open our understanding of how the physical universe was created through an interweaving of Light and the "Music of the Spheres." Music, a vibrant, colorful language, can help us elevate our consciousness and awareness, widening our field of understanding of how we are part of a greater reality, and that sound is an integral part of who we are and how we got here—it is the sacred song of the soul.

Not surprisingly, we humans are still on uncertain ground when attempting to define our own intelligence. Music research is showing us that we still lack a proper framework for understanding the true nature of music and sound potential. Without expanding our knowledge through new technology and an open-minded awareness, we cannot fully grasp our own presence as energy embodiments.

The study of sound is so vast—researchers and scientists will continue to share their findings that involve everything from interspecies' communication to health and healing, to our place in the universe, thus deepening our understanding. It is difficult in any field of science to change the existing scientific paradigm and its associated language, but when we gain the language to describe the importance of sound, we will be able to find our place as part of a greater whole, as one of many instruments within the greater orchestration of Life.

Whether we are able to recognize it or not, the myriads of levels of sound waves will continue to connect us with the vibratory life of plants, animals and the intelligence surrounding us, for human resonance is part of a larger, natural cosmo-physical symphony.

We share with all creation a vibratory Garden of Life, and even plants and animals have given us great insights into the power of sounds to create linkages between us. If we could communicate with everything from spiritual entities to plants through these vibratory fields, and if plants have the ability to "think," could we not devise common strategies to talk to higher levels of non-human life with natural sound technology built inside our body and mind, i.e., musical cybernetics?

In our Garden of Life, we live within bio-music that brings forth bio-geometry, allowing for paraphysical communication over great distances using particular sounds, as seen in the communication amongst whales. Rather than seeing others in our Garden of Life as being on the lower chain-of-evolution, as "a sub-kingdom," we should recognize and honor all creation as we use sound communication to share with each other as co-participants in this Life.

Science and cymatics have shown us that sound is form and form is sound, and Emoto demonstrated how our thoughts and music affect the geometries of Life within us. Water is the key here, and we are composed of at least 65% water. So, it is up to us to make it beautiful using the vibrations of our thoughts and voices. Sound pictures and sacred geometries can help us integrate our vision of humanity with our spiritual and ecological insights so that humans can emerge as integrated beings fully engaged in a vast spectrum of light and frequencies of energy working for the transformation of our body, mind, and soul. Perhaps, the most valuable inspiration we can take from this understanding is how sound works within us, as the "Universal Tone" in a myriad of ways and conversations.

If we can grasp this awareness via our feelings and express the fuller vibratory signal ranges, beginning to use the sequences of sounds and vibrations, we can live a holistic life with a more promising future that will flow into us from the living soundscapes being forged. Whether we are sitting at home, in the Great Pyramid, in any sacred building or in Nature, we can resonate loudly or in vibratory silence to find the power to reach into a greater Divine state of Consciousness. The frequencies are there for healing and guiding our physical bodies back to the true perfect Nature as One with the Godhead.

As we are all different sparks of the Divine, we each have our own frequencies and vibrations of higher resonance. The more we see ourselves as energy vibratory bodies, the more we can heal ourselves and see how to keep the music of Love living in our hearts and minds, a vibratory medicine that is able to transform our reality. We are part of the symphony of the Divine—let us take the time to listen!

ENDNOTES

1. Measures, M.P., & Weinberger, P. (1970). The effect of four audible sound frequencies on the growth of Marquis spring wheat. *Botany, 48*, 659-662.

2. Gagliano, M., Renton, M., Duvdevani, N., Timmins, M., & Mancuso, S. (2012). Acoustic and magnetic communication in plants: Is it possible?. *Plant Signaling & Behavior, 7*(10), 1346–1348. https://doi.org/10.4161/psb.21517

3. Jenny's findings were expressed in cps (cycles per second) which is the same as Hz (Hertz), where 1 cps = 1 Hz, and his books showed results from a variety of frequencies throughout the range of human hearing.

4. Kepler's Third Law states that the squares of the orbital periods of the planets are directly proportional to the cubes of the semi-major axes of their orbits ($P^2 = a^3$). Accordingly, the relation between the orbital period (T) of a planet around the sun and its mean distance (r) from the sun is A. r3/T3 = constant. T2 = R3, where T is the planet's orbital period in years and R is a planet's distance from the sun in Astronomical Units (AU).

5. Akimoto, K., Hu, A., Yamaguchi, T. and Kobayashi, H. (2018) Effect of 528 Hz Music on the Endocrine System and Autonomic Nervous System. *Health*, 10, 1159-1170. doi: 10.4236/health.2018.109088.

6. Zhang, J., Harbottle, G., Wang, C., & Kong, Z. (1999). Oldest playable musical instruments found at Jiahu early Neolithic site in China. *Nature, 401*(6751), 366–368. https://doi.org/10.1038/43865

7. Hurtak, J.J. (1973) *The Book of Knowledge: The Keys of Enoch*®. Los Gatos: Academy For Future Science. keysofenoch.org

MEET OUR SACRED STORYTELLERS

DEBORAH ANN BUSTIN continues her lifelong love affair with the power of words to process life's biggest questions, heal wounds, inspire hope, create laughter, and move people's hearts. Onward! Upward!

JEAN FITZGERALD CANALE is an artist, musician, gardener, novice chef, rebel, and student of mysticism. She has a passion for learning, creating, and exploring the fabric of life and consciousness.

DARREN CURTIS AND BRADLEY PITT are music producers, composers, sound artists, and spiritual educators. For the past 20 years, this team has developed immersive experiences and multi-media sound installations as unique forms of experimental and meditative music that merge art and consciousness. They have crafted numerous sacred music albums and produced international award-winning multimedia films. sacredresonance.com.au.

DONCY FALVEY is an Usui Shiki Ryoho reiki master, animal reiki master, chakra healing master, color and crystal therapist, sound therapy and healing practitioner, master meditation teacher, and ordained minister. Doncy currently lives amongst the Red Rocks of Arizona and is spearheading the prospects of a conscious living community.

JOHN PAUL (EAGLE HEART) FISCHBACH is a theatre and film director, and an initiated shaman, sacred pipe carrier and site whisperer. His documentary series, *The Shaman and the Stones,* is currently in production. eagleheart. com.au.

ULRIKE GRANÖGGER teaches *The Keys of Enoch*® and lectures on science, consciousness, and personal spirituality. She studied the effects of the "Kozyrev Mirror" and the "Wave Genome" and regularly contributes to Catherine Austin Fitt's Solari Report. science.solari.com.

BETH GREEN is an intuitively-guided counselor, teacher, author, composer, and pianist. Born in 1945, she had a spiritual and psychic awakening in 1980, and since then has helped countless people with her counseling, workshops, books, music, talks, and more. You can access her books, blogs, videos, and music for free at healingartsnetwork.org.

STEVEN HALPERN is a Grammy® nominated recording artist, composer, producer, and pioneering sound healer. His music has touched the lives of millions around the world, manifesting his soul's mission of bringing more inner peace and harmony onto the planet. stevenhalpernmusic.com

DR. JOANNE HALVERSON lived off-grid in the woods. She is a psychotherapist and soul mentor. Coast Salish shamans entrusted her with initiations, teachings, and medicine names-Ancient Spirit Person and an ancient Samish name. Gifts of wisdom are to be shared. thrivecounselorseattle.com.

MICHELLE ANNE HOBART is an integrative energy medicine practitioner, and spiritual emergence coach. She supports those in spiritual emergence who have experienced NDE, kundalini awakening, and psychic opening. michelleannehobart.com.

ALLISON KENNY is a featured author and contributor for the award-winning publishing division of 360° NATION. Her work explores divine beauty and encounters with the unknown. She is aunt and godmother to her beloved niece, Rachel, aunt to her beloved niece, Autumn, and to her beloved nephews, Austin and Colton.

TAMARA KNOX M.MSC, D.D., is an international bestselling author and a devotee to the Light. She uses breath, sound, movement, consciousness, and food energetics to explore metaphysical and multidimensional realms. shekhinahpath.com.

DONNA KUEBLER is a world traveler and multi-dimensional healer who clears dark karma to restore one back to wholeness. She's a channel, seer, shaman, Melchizedek priest, and sound healer who sings with the angels so that you can feel, happy, whole, holy, and at peace. thegoldenalchemist.com.

DEBRA LAFOREST completed training at the Center for Neuroacoustic Research. She has been a pioneer Vibroacoustic Practitioner in day spas, and clinical and private practice since 2001.

MICHELLE MCCLENNEN graduated from Delphi University, a renowned mystery school for psychic development. She uses her intuitive skills as a spiritual counselor, oracle reader, and energy healer. michellemcclennen. com.

PAMELA NANCE has a graduate degree in cultural anthropology, minor degrees in archaeology and religion, and a 30-year career in social and biostatistical sciences. Pamela has researched the survival of consciousness after death for over 30 years and has obtained certifications in healing touch, past life regression, shamanism, and spiritual dowsing. pamelanance.com.

ELIJAH NEGASI was born and raised in the Bronx borough of New York City.

RON THOMAS is a guy with basic guitar and singing skills, who took a Romp Down Memory Lane with dementia patients–an encore career in the spirit of healing and service.

DEVARA THUNDERBEAT is a multi–award winning musician and composer. She is an author, teacher, speaker, 22 DNA activator, reiki master, and pioneer in sound healing. thunderbeat.com.

JEFFREY E. WASHER has been a master electrician in the field of electrical construction for over 30 years. He has also invented products, written, performed, and produced music and now is writing short stories to help people.

SARYON MICHAEL WHITE and his partner Daisy specialize in helping select the right crystal alchemy bowl or personalized set of musically tuned bowls, to complement your unique journey and amplify the gifts of your sacred work. Finding the right bowls is an intuitive process of finding a resonant match. crystalalchemybowls.com.

DIANE WILCOXSON is a singer, orator, oracle, and certified sound healer. She is a master on a masterful journey with sound, light, love, and laughter. miraclesofmastery.com.

DIANE WILCOXSON AND MEGAN WAGNER are co-founders of The Mastery Project. Together they pioneer mastery journeys, adventures, and tools and processes for personal and collective mastery and thriving while living one's soul blueprint. ancientfuture.today.

MEET OUR AUTHORS

JAMES J. HURTAK, Ph.D., Ph.D. and DESIREE HURTAK, Ph.D. are Social Scientists, composers, authors, and futurists. Dr. J.J. Hurtak is the author of the best-seller *The Book of Knowledge: The Keys of Enoch*®⁷, translated into twenty-five languages. He has Ph.Ds from the University of California and the University of Minnesota. Together, the Hurtaks are the founders of The Academy For Future Science, an international NGO.

They have written numerous books together that include *Salvator Mundi, The Seventy-Two Holy Names of The Myriad Names of the Divine Mother, The Overself Awakening, Pistis Sophia: Text and Commentary*, a commentary on *The Gospel of Mary* and more. Drs. Hurtak are co-authors of *Mind Dynamics in Space and Time* (2016), with the collaboration of world-renowned physicist, Dr. Elizabeth Rauscher, encompassing the rigorous scientific research of remote viewing and consciousness. They are also well known for their inspirational music, including their CD *Sacred Name Sacred Codes* which is a collaborative music with Steven Halpern, and their latest album with Steven entitled *Sacred Cyphers of the Divine Mother*. Dr. J.J. Hurtak's work has been performed by the German Symphonic Orchestra of Berlin (2011) with the famous singer Jocelyn Smith. Dr. J.J. Hurtak was also cowriter and composer with legendry song writer Alice Coltrane, and their work was presented at the New Jersey Center for Performing Arts (*New York Times*, 2006) where Desiree performed with the chorus. Their music of sacred mantras has been performed and sung throughout Europe and Latin America. Together, Drs. Hurtak continue to introduce music, having over 30 albums to date, to help unify cultures within the larger global society.

Drs. Hurtak are also well-known as pioneers in Acoustic Archaeology having done music testing in many of the Mayan Temples, as well as the Great Pyramid of Giza. They were part of the team that discovered the "Tomb of Osiris" on the Giza Plateau in 1997. Their most recent publications to which they have been contributors are, *Our Moment of Choice* (2020), which includes their insights on consciousness together with those of over forty other internationally respected writers, such as Dr. Deepak Chopra and Dr. Bruce Lipton, and *Making Contact* (2021) with chapters by Nick Pope and Linda Moulton Howe, and *The Holomovement: Embracing Our Collective Purpose To Unite Humanity* (2023), which explores various inspirational understandings of the living universe and our integral place in its evolution.

J.J. Hurtak was a member of the founding faculty at California Institute of the Arts. Together the Hurtaks have won fifteen awards at national and international film festivals for their numerous animated and graphic arts films regarding the exploration of higher consciousness with the following titles: *Merkabah* (1997), *The Light Body* (2002), *Initiation* (2004), *The Voice of Africa* (2013), and *Gates of Light* (2014).

Their lectures have introduced the common goals of spiritual understanding, science, and sustainable development. Drs. Hurtak have appeared on *Netflix, BBC Radio, Gaia TV, Coast-to-Coast AM* radio programs,

Deepak Chopra's *Wellness Radio, Hay House Radio,* to mention a few. They have given conferences at many universities. Their lectures, seminars, and musical events have been attended by world leaders, educators, and their scientific colleagues. Together, they are members of the Evolutionary Leaders group that constitutes a body of speakers and writers from around the world who are shaping the shift in consciousness around the world towards a positive future.

You can find them on their websites: keysofenoch.org and futurescience.org

Printed in Great Britain
by Amazon

41641430R00131